The Frugal Oenophile's Winegrape Primer

by Richard Best

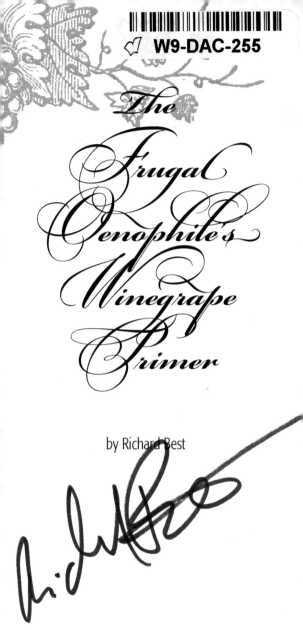

Chester Press

Also by Richard Best

The Frugal Oenophile's Lexicon of Wine Tasting Terms,
ISBN: 0-965046-5-5. This best-selling book on wine language
is available at many wineries and bookstores or directly from
www.frugalwine.com.

The Frugal Oenophile's Lexicon of Wine Tasting Terms –
Japanese Edition, ISBN: 0-965046-6-3. The original Lexicon,
translated to the highest standard. Both English and Japanese
terms are included, along with Katakana where appropriate,
with definitions in Japanese.

The Frugal Oenophile on Wine & Grapes, ISBN 0-9685046-7-1.
This 48-page booklet gathers together all the grape features that
appeared in The Frugal Oenophile newsletter. Each profile tells
the story of the grape and the wine, with historical context and
current application.

The Frugal Oenophile's Compleat Home Winetasting Kit
contains everything you need to plan and host a winetasting
for friends or colleagues: flight sheets, note booklets, helpful
tip sheets, "how to" booklet, and more. All you need to add is
wine, food and a few friends.

The Frugal Oenophile's Educational Wine Newsletter
features educational articles on the many interesting aspects
of wine, making wine, living with wine, and more. By email
subscription.

The Frugal Oenophile's Wine of the Week Blog
(tfo-wow.blogspot.com), features wines that are as easy on the
pocket book as they are on the palate.

www.frugalwine.com

Contents

A Remarkable Fruit, the Grape

The grapevine is a remarkable plant. Left to its own inclinations, it will grow and climb as far and as high as it can. Single grapevines have been known to cover as much as an entire acre. And their root systems are just as impressive, reaching 15 metres or more into the most inhospitable soils.

Grapevines are Temperate Zone plants. They like heat and can tolerate cold, but not too much of either. The happy grapevine is a master of adapting and of surviving, and it rewards earth's creatures with its luscious grapes, which birds, animals and hominids have enjoyed for millions of years.

The modern winegrape, however, is quite a different character. It too wants to grow unrestrained, and in doing so it pours its energy into canes and foliage, not into grapes. But winemakers want grapes, often as many of them as possible. Interestingly, the vine readily co-operates if treated correctly. Planted in less desirable areas, the plant struggles to gain a foothold. Deprived of an easy source of water, it drives its roots deep into the land, extracting a complex mix of microchemical nutrients, perhaps the very elements that account for "terroir". If the vine is pruned, it fights back by producing a richer crop of grapes. And if the crop and the foliage are thinned, the plant puts more energy – and goodness – into the grapes that remain.

This is the pattern that viniculturalists, the people who grow winegrapes, have practiced for generations: plant on land that's too poor for any other crop; stress the vines by planting densely; withhold water; and mercilessly prune and thin. A grape variety that wants to produce 8 tons/acre of mediocre fruit can thus be coaxed into producing 2-3 tons/acre of excellent winegrapes.

This book contains brief descriptions of nearly 250 grapes – a far cry from the thousands of varieties that are routinely used to produce wine world-wide – plus some token coverage of regions and styles. To document every grape would be impossible, and perhaps foolhardy. I've tried to include all of the grape varieties that you might find on or in a wine bottle. In the case of Old World wines, I've tried to shed light on the grapes that you have probably already encountered but may not yet know by name. Burgundy is a classic case. Many people enjoy Red Burgundy and Pinot Noir, but have never made the connection between the two, or between White Burgundy and Chardonnay – or between Chianti and Sangiovese, for that matter.

My hope is that this guide will help you to discover more wines. Knowing, for example, that Condrieu is made from Viognier may be just the information a Viognier lover needs to try Condrieu and vice versa. And knowing that Carménère was once taken for Merlot may motivate a Merlot fan to try a Chilean delight.

Varieties, Clones & Cultivars

The job of the ampelographer has always been a difficult one. As soon as these grape researchers get a handle on one variety, someone throws a wrinkle in with a new crossing or a new-found variety. With more than 3000 winegrapes currently in use and thousands more on the sidelines, ampelographers are kept busy trying to determine the origin and precise parentage of each grape.

Our best guess is that winegrapes were cultivated by early Eastern Europeans and Eurasians at least 10,000 years ago. Ever since, grape growers have selected the best tasting and most productive plants for their vineyards. The more adventurous types would regularly cross one variety with another to create a new species that they hoped would show the best qualities of the parents. This practice has been going on for so long – long before any sort of record keeping – that the majority of today's species are of "unknown origin". It is only with the use of DNA analysis that scientists can begin to unravel the mystery of how any one grape came about.

The practice of cross-breeding varieties yields more misses than hits, and yet in the case of winegrapes we've somehow managed to create thousands of sub-species, all different and all capable of producing wine with at least some merit.

Grapes belong to the genus of plants called Vitaceae and the genera Vitis. Individual grape species in any quantity appear to be unique to the Northern Hemisphere, with only a couple of varieties native to the Southern Hemisphere, principally in Southeast Asia.

The grape family that dominates Europe is the species Vinifera – the wine-making grape. Was it always so or did other varieties slowly die out in favour of the Vinifera? We don't know. Most of the winegrape varieties that we are familiar with today are from the Vinifera family: Cabernet, Chardonnay, Gamay, Tempranillo, and a host of others. Properly speaking, we would call the Muscat grape, for example, "Vitis Vinifera Muscat".

North America has far more grape species – about 60. Sadly, the majority are unsuitable for wine production. Before the discovery of phylloxera, attempts to plant the better Vinifera grapes failed in North America. It was only when the vines were grafted onto North American rootstocks that the Vinifera grapes were able to survive. So we now see the same classic European vinifera grapes growing in North America and throughout the world.

When two plants from the same species are crossed, the result can be unpredictable. The goal is to combine the positive characteristics of two known grapes. When successful, as when Cabernet Franc was crossed with Sauvignon Blanc to create Cabernet Sauvignon, the result can literally change the face of the industry. Other times the cross is merely adequate, as in the case of the unexceptional Optima, which is the offspring of "Sylvaner x Riesling" and Müller-Thurgau. A grape variety with only Vinifera parents is called a Cross.

When two different grape species are crossed, for example the Vinifera Folle Blanche and North American Riperia, the resulting vine is called a Hybrid or Interspecific Cross, in this case Baco Noir. These grapes often solve two problems: phylloxera susceptibility and the so-called "foxy" taste so common in wines made from North American grapes. The North American genes provide the resistance to many diseases as well as phylloxera, while the Vinifera genes provide the type of flavour we've come to expect in better quality wines.

Crossing and hybridization of cultivars (cultivated varieties) are long and complicated processes. Sometimes it takes many generations of crossings to create a single useful cultivar. Francois Baco, for example, created roughly 7000 new grape varieties in his lifetime, yet only the Baco Noir and Baco Blanc emerged as useful cultivars.

Grapevines are grown from cuttings for a number of reasons. Cuttings ensure consistency, since each new vine is a "clone" of the original, whereas growing vines from seeds is unpredictable. Grapevines also need resistant rootstock and so are almost always grafted onto North American or Hybrid rootstocks, which eliminates a lot of risks. There is also a tendency for some grapes to mutate, although mutations can be a good thing; Pinot Blanc and Pinot Gris, for example, are mutations of Pinot Noir.

The Curse of "Varietalism"

There is a tradition in the classic European wine regions of naming the wine after the place where it was grown: Barolo comes from Barolo; Rioja comes from Rioja. After hundreds and sometimes thousands of years of growing and refining, the locals simply understood that the best possible grapes had been decided on, and so, technically, it was redundant to say that Hermitage was made from Syrah: the two are one and the same. Labelling systems evolved to proclaim the location – the region, the vineyard or the chateau – rather than the underlying grape(s).

For those who grew up with the concept, it worked well enough. But as wine markets expanded, the system presented problems. How was someone browsing a wine shelf somewhere in rural Canada to know, for example, that Bourgueil is made from Cabernet Franc? It's so much easier, and perhaps safer, to buy the bottle that has Cabernet Franc written right on the label.

Varietal naming – putting the grape name on the label – is not new, but the real push came from the American wine writer and importer Frank Schoonmaker, who aggressively promoted the use of varietal names for New World wines. A Cabernet varietal is always Cabernet, no matter where it was grown. Schoonmaker's approach helped wine drinkers to get a handle on wine, and unlocked some of its mystery. Varietal naming caught on rapidly in the New World, and in fact non-varietally named wines are becoming a bit of an oddity. The reason for this success is the simplicity of varietal naming, and in a market that suffers from a surfeit of complexity, consumers welcomed the more user-friendly approach.

But there is a downside – what I call varietal-ism. Reliance on grape name alone has led the average wine drinker to assume that grape variety is all that matters (if in fact they even know that it's a grape name on the label). So instead of discovering new wines, people too often latch onto a single grape name. How often do we hear a wine drinker proclaim, *13*

"I only drink Merlot"? To embrace one grape so completely denies the wealth of variety and enjoyment that other grape varieties provide.

Varietalism also suggests to the consumer that wines are pure products. However, most wine regions allow blending of as much as 25% "other" grapes in a varietal. So that bottle of Merlot could be up to 25% any blending grape. There also can be a world of difference between wines made from the same grape in different parts of the world. As well, we should keep in mind that some of the greatest wines are blends of different grapes: Bordeaux, Rioja, Chianti, Châteauneuf-du-Pape, and many, many others. Blending is an important skill in the winemaker's arsenal, and its significance should not be underestimated.

Most of us would hate to have the same meal every night. We like variety, and we love to experience new taste delights. Limiting our wine selections to a single label, brand, grape or region robs us of the discovery of the almost infinite variety of wines that are available today. Instead, let's embrace the rich palette of grapes and grape blends that have satisfied a world full of wine drinkers for countless generations.

About This Book

The main section of this primer is devoted to winegrapes and wine styles. The first line of each entry gives the grape or region name, often with a pronunciation guide (if pronunciation isn't obvious), and occasionally a synonym or two, followed by whether the term is a grape variety, an appellation name or a wine style. This is followed by the grape or wine's story in brief, the characteristics of the wine and, finally, a few food matching suggestions.

You'll notice that some grapes have a lot of detail while others have as little as a single sentence. The material available on winegrapes tends to favour the well-known grapes while neglecting the less well known. Rather than follow the established pattern of over- and under-exposure, I've tried to provide a useful amount of information while keeping the descriptions short. In some cases, it was difficult to distil the mass of information into a single paragraph. (Do we really need another six pages on Chardonnay?) In other cases, there was very little information to draw on. I've included what I could, and can only offer to continue looking for data on some of the more obscure grapes.

Within the text, I have substituted the word Hybrid for the word Variety when the grape is a French Hybrid. I do this to draw attention to the often unappreciated Hybrid grapes that are not only every bit as good as many of the Vinifera grapes, but which also make viticulture possible in marginal areas such as Great Britain and Eastern Canada. References to other entries in the book are set in *italics*.

In the Appendix you'll find a brief summary of the European countries and wine regions that use appellation names rather than grape names. This will give you some idea of where to look for the winegrapes you may be fond of, or for new wines for you to try.

Lastly is a list of wine terms (taken from my wine Lexicon).

Richard Best

Winegrapes

A - Z

■ Airén (eye-REN) VARIETY

Airén is the world's most abundantly planted winegrape. Found almost exclusively in Spain, especially in La Mancha and Valdepeñas, it finds its way into roughly 90% of all Spanish white wines and is sometimes blended into red wines. Widely used in Spanish "brandy", Airén can yield an acceptable, even good, dry wine if carefully vinted, although the majority is rather dull. Interest is currently waning. (A.k.a. Manchega, Valdepeña Blanca.)

Descriptors Mildly aromatic, fruity, light, crisp and fresh with medium body and high alcohol. Somewhat neutral in character and may sometimes show some oxidation.

Food Matches SEE VINHO VERDE.

■ Albana (all-BA-nuh) VARIETY

Found mainly in Emilia-Romagna, this ancient and normally banal grape produces a decent varietal wine, somewhat like Pinot Blanc, if carefully cropped and vinified. It can be dry, off-dry or sweet, and works well with pasta, cream sauces and seafoods.

■ Aligoté (ah-lee-goh-tay) VARIETY

Grown in Burgundy and its subregion *Chablis* since the 16th century, Aligoté is considered to be *Chardonnay's* poorer cousin in the form of Aligoté de Bourgogne. It can result in a very good wine – even excellent in good years, if ripe – but is as often simple, tart and thin. Sometimes made into a sparkling wine, and it is the basis of "kir". Also found in Chile, California and Eastern Europe, especially Bulgaria and Romania, and Canada. Not as common as it once was.

Descriptors Nutty, lemon, buttermilk and pine aromas; crisp and slightly tart. Most is early drinking; better examples can improve for a couple of years at most.

Food Matches Chicken wings, shrimp, scallops, oysters, mussels, cod, trout, grilled sole, prawns, brie, Spanish tortilla, spring rolls, escargot, frog legs.

■ Alvarinho/Albariño

(all-var-REE-noh/all-bar-REE-nyoh)   **VARIETY**

Widely used in the Rios do Minho region of Portugal to make white Vinho Verde, this grape, as Albarino, produces a high quality *Viognier*-like wine in Spain, but is little known elsewhere. Sometimes appears as a varietal, and can be rather expensive.

Descriptors   Highly fragrant, with aromas of apricot, peach, grapefruit and sometimes a hint of *Muscat*. Fairly light bodied with fresh, crisp acidity, low to medium alcohol and a creamy texture.

Food Matches   Seafoods, especially scallops. Also SEE VINHO VERDE.

■ Arinto/Perdañao (ah-RIN-toh/per-DAN-yoh) **VARIETY**

Found in Portugal, mainly in the central region, this is the region's top "noble" white grape, producing quality wines in that country's hot climate. As Perdañao, it is important in the production of Vinho Verde.

Descriptors   Aromatic with aromas of citrus, peach, possibly oak, and high acidity. Has some ageing ability.

Food Matches   SEE VINHO VERDE.

■ Arneis (ar-NAYS) **VARIETY**

Found almost exclusively near Alba in Piedmont, Italy, Arneis produces a limited number of wine styles ranging from dry to sweet. Rather scarce, although Australia is experimenting with it. The wine does not age well and can be pricey. Sometimes called Barolo Bianco.

Descriptors   Aromas of apple, pear, anise, perfume, herbs, and almond. Typically dry with low acidity.

Food Matches   Pasta with cream sauce, whitefish, onion tart.

■ Assyrtico/Assyrtiko (a-SEER-TEE-koh) **VARIETY**

Important in Greece, especially the Isle of Santinori where the grape produces versatile wines with good character, quality and substance, and some ageing ability. Equally important as a blending grape. (Also SEE VIN SANTO.)

Descriptors   Lime, honeysuckle, green apple, "steel", mineral and herbs, with good acidity and body.

Food Matches   Seafoods.

■ Asti Spumante (ah-STEE spoo-MAHN-teh)   STYLE

A popular light sparkling wine made from *Muscat* in the Piedmont region of Italy. Moscato d'Asti is similar but with less effervescence and lower alcohol (about 5%). Typically made by the bulk or Charmat Method.

Descriptors   Fresh, light, usually grapey, with good mousse and body. Often medium-sweet and may be low in alcohol. Best within its first year.

Food Matches   Zabaglione, strawberry fool, summer afternoons.

■ Auxerrois (oaks-AIR-wah/oh-SAIR-wah)   VARIETY

Grown mostly in Alsace and Burgundy, Auxerrois can be rich and exciting or bland and flabby. Sometimes called Pinot Auxerrois and once thought to be related to *Chardonnay,* it may be added to *Edelswicker.* New World Auxerrois can be racy and flavourful, and it is very food friendly. (*Malbec,* a red grape, is sometimes called Auxerrois.)

Descriptors   Dry and citrusy with high acid and alcohol, though medium-bodied. Can resemble *Pinot Blanc* when young or *Chablis* when aged. Sweet versions can be honey-like. Not usually oaked.

Food Matches   Grilled or roasted poultry, sushi, lobster, crab, pasta with cream sauce, poached chicken, trout, risotto.

■ Avesso (a-VAY-so)   VARIETY

One of the Vinho Verde grapes, showing good aroma, low acid and good body, although it can be a bit rustic.

■ Bacchus   VARIETY

Named after the Roman god of revelry, Bacchus is a cross of "Riesling x Sylvaner" and *Müller-Thurgau.* Found in cooler climates, especially Germany's Mosel and Franken, and also popular in England, it produces an early sipping wine that is never oaked because of its delicacy. Sometimes blended with Müller-Thurgau and other grapes to produce *Liebfraumilch.*

Descriptors   Highly aromatic with muscat-like perfume and tropical fruit aromas. Dry to off-dry with low acidity and good body. Similar to Müller-Thurgau, though showing less overall quality. Best from 1-3 years.

Food Matches   Mild fish, Chinese. ALSO SEE MÜLLER-THURGAU.

■ Beajolais Blanc   APPELLATION

SEE CHARDONNAY.

■ Bical (BEE-sal)   VARIETY

Found principally in the Bairrada and Dao regions of Portugal, Bical has the peculiar distinction of being called Borrado das Moscas (fly droppings) because of its appearance, not its vinous prospects. Mainly used for blending, especially in sparkling wines.

Descriptors   Soapy, flowery, with crisp acidity and high alcohol, showing honey aromas after a few years in bottle.

■ Blanc Fumé (blahN foo-may)   STYLE

A name given to *Sauvignon Blanc* in the Central Loire village of Pouilly-sur-Loire, and the inspiration for California's *Fumé Blanc*. More often called Pouilly-Fumé, these wines are not oaked; fumé (smoky) refers to the wine's flinty quality, which is believed to come from the soil the vines grow in.

■ Boal/Bual (boo-ahl)   VARIETY

At one time an important grape on the Island of Madeira, where it produces Madeira in a "Boal" style. Could make a comeback there as regulations now require a minimum percentage of the Boal grape. Also found in mainland Portugal. Sometimes called Boal Branco.

Descriptors   Similar to "Malmsey", a type of Madeira, with less colour and richness.

■ Bordeaux Blanc   STYLE/APPELLATION

The dry white wines of Bordeaux are blended from *Semillon, Sauvignon Blanc* and *Muscadelle*. Although often hard to find, the wines usually offer very good value and tend to express the characteristics of the Sauvignon Blanc, with a bit of heft courtesy of the Semillon, and a fresh, fruity note from the Muscadelle. (Also SEE ENTRE-DEUX-MERS, MERITAGE, SAUTERNES.)

■ Bourboulenc   VARIETY

Possibly a Greek ex-patriot, this ancient grape was once found throughout France's Southern Rhône, Provence and the Midi. One of the accepted grapes in *Châteauneuf-du-Pape,* it today is found mainly in Corbiéres and Minervois blends. On its own it rarely rises above mediocre.

■ Bourgogne (Blanc)/White Burgundy   APPELLATION

Although *Chablis* and *Beaujolais* are part of Burgundy, white burgundy proper comes exclusively from the Cote d'Or and the Cote de Nuit, and may be made only from *Chardonnay.* Considered to be the model for great Chardonnay. (Also SEE ALIGOTÉ.)

■ Catarratto   VARIETY

An important white grape in Sicily, second only to *Trebbiano,* and also found throughout Italy, Catarratto was once used to produce Marsala. It shows good aroma and acidity if yields are kept in check and vinification is well handled. Now finding its way into varietal blends, such as Catarratto-Chardonnay, to good effect.

Descriptors Good body, acid and aroma; slightly tart.
Food Matches Quiche, roast chicken, full-bodied ocean fish.
ALSO SEE CHARDONNAY.

■ Catawba (cuh-TAW-buh)   HYBRID

This pink-skinned grape can be found throughout the southern and eastern US, especially New York State. Likely the chance offspring of some Vinifera grape and *Labrusca,* it was once popular as a "blush" wine and, depending on the degree of skin colour, can even approach red. Very good as a Late Harvest wine, although it always shows a bit of foxy character.

■ Cava (KAH-vah)   STYLE

The name given to Spanish sparkling wines made using the traditional method. Crisp, flavourful and high quality, Cava is made mainly from the traditional grapes Xerel-lo, *Parellada,* and *Macabeo,* although *Chardonnay* is beginning to creep into high-end blends. As well as a good stand-in for champagne, Cava is excellent with Szechwan and Thai dishes.

■ **Cerceal/Sercial** (sair-see-al)   VARIETY

Possibly a descendent of *Riesling,* Cerceal is important in Portugal for the production of Madeira. It also produces a light, dry, delicate table wine that is suitable for ageing.

■ **Chablis** (sha-blee)   APPELLATION

This subregion of Burgundy lies about a 2-hour drive southeast of Paris, and produces a white wine of the same name from *Chardonnay* grapes. Because of a cooler climate, Chablis wines are light to medium in body, tense and stoney, and can be austere and dumb in their youth. Usually vinted in stainless steel or old oak, Chablis is one of the most age-worthy white wines – up to 10 years – and can be quite pricey. (For a time, the name was appropriated for generic white blends in much of the New World.) ALSO SEE ALIGOTÉ.

Descriptors   Citrus, apple and flinty or steely aromas; crisp, deep and rarely with any evidence of oak, although that is changing. (SEE CHARDONNAY.)

Food Matches   A good match for seafood especially oysters, smoked salmon, sole, clam chowder, tempura.

■ **Champagne** (sham-payn/sham-pan-yuh) APPELLATION

This wine region in north-eastern France is known for its high quality sparkling wines made from *Chardonnay* and the red grapes *Pinot Noir* and *Pinot Meunier.* Considered by many to be the greatest sparkling wines, although a number of regions are nipping at Champagne's heels. The majority is non-vintage but vintages are often "declared" in exceptional years. (The name was appropriated by New World winemakers and still appears on the labels of many non-French sparkling wines.)

Descriptors   Fruity aromas are usually accompanied by toasty, biscuity notes from extended lees ageing. Intensely fine, dense and long-lived mousse. Can age up to five years or more after release, whether vintage or non-vintage.

Food Matches   Hors d'oeuvre, desserts, hot tubs.

■ **Chancellor**   HYBRID

This cold-hardy French Hybrid once produced quality red and rosé wines in its native France, but is no longer found there. It has now found good homes in Canada and parts of the eastern and central US, producing red wines of good quality.

■ **Chardonnay** (shar-duh-nay)   **VARIETY**

Often called the "King of the white grapes", Chardonnay produces wines that range from fair to extraordinary. Valued for its body, versatility, ease of growth and market share, it is usually best within 1-3 years, although Old World types can age 6 years or more. Look also for barrel fermented, barrel aged, or sur lie. Often treated to malolactic fermentation to yield a buttery quality. In Australia, it is sometimes blended with *Semillon*. Chardonnay is the grape used in *Chablis,* Bourgogne Blanc, *Beajolais Blanc,* Pouilly Fuissé, Blanc De Blancs *Champagne,* Montrachet, and a host of others.

Descriptors   Medium to full bodied dry wines show aromas of apple, pear and tropical fruits, a creamy palate and low acidity. Oaked versions also show vanilla, nuts, toast, and butter.

Food Matches   Camembert, carbonnara sauce, cheddar, chicken Kiev, cream sauces, deep-fried fish, duck, egg dishes, emmenthal, gruyere, guacamole, hollandaise, lobster, Monterey jack, mushrooms, pork tenderloin, salmon, shellfish, squash, tarragon, trout, turkey, veal.

■ **Chardonnay Musqué** (c. muss-KAY)   **VARIETY**

This interesting mutation of the Chardonnay grape shows an attractive musky aroma. Very much a Chardonnay, with good body and full flavour. Not usually oaked and sometimes called, simply, "Chardonnay Unoaked" in New World wines.

Descriptors   The body and texture of Chardonnay, with lemon and apple aromas and an inviting Muscat-like undertone.

Food Matches   Flavourful fish, any style of poultry, roast pork.

■ **Chardonnel/Chardonel**   **HYBRID**

A newer hybrid of *Chardonnay* and *Seyval* Blanc that some see as the "great white hope" of lesser-known and cooler US wine regions. Produces a respectable dry, full-bodied wine without any foxy character. Can be high quality.

Descriptors   Bears a strong resemblance to Chardonnay, though with a little less character.

Food Matches   See Chardonnay.

■ Chasselas (shas-lah) VARIETY

One of the oldest known grapes, Chasselas is another example of terroir at work. Thought to have originated in Egypt, Chasselas is now found mainly in Central France, Alsace and the Loire regions, where it makes light, somewhat neutral and uninteresting table wines, and also in Germany where it is called *Gütedel*. In Switzerland, however, it is one of their best varieties, producing excellent table wines under the Fendant varietal name. Also used as a table grape, it is not as popular as it once was.

Descriptors Light, fresh and crisp, with light floral, mineral, citrus and almond aromas, sometimes with a light prickle. Best in its first two years of life.

Food Matches Crab, clam sauce, cheese fondue, oka, raclette.

■ Chenin Blanc/Steen (sheh-nan blahN) VARIETY

Known since the 9th century, the best examples are from France and especially the Loire Valley, where Chenin makes Anjou, Saumur and several types of Vouvray. Versatile but often unexceptional, ranging from dry to sweet to sparkling, late harvest, TBA, and "sherry". It is the number one white grape of South Africa, where it was for a long time called Steen. Although not a Pinot grape, it is sometimes called Pineau de Loire. Also grown successfully in California's Central Valley, Chenin is very food friendly and sweeter versions can age exceptionally well.

Descriptors Aromas can include honey, peaches, unripe apples, fig, quince and melon, with grassy, nutty or herbaceous notes. Light to medium bodied and concentrated, with bracing acidity and sometimes an oily texture. Best from 3 to 30 years.

Food Matches Apple/prune stuffing, asiago, camembert, chévre, chicken with pineapple, curry, cream sauces, lobster, monterey jack, oysters, roast pork, roasted or broiled poultry, Swiss cheese, trout, quiche, chicken livers.

Late Harvest Fruit or almond pudding.

■ Clairette (Blanche)   VARIETY

Found mainly in Southern France, this little-used grape is often the base for vermouth and sparkling wines or as a blending grape. It can also appear in *Châtauneuf-du-Pape*. Called Blanquette in Australia, interest is waffling at this time. (Not to be confused with Clairette de Languedoc, a light red wine.)

Descriptors Rather plain, with high alcohol and low acid. Oxidyzes easily.

■ Colombar/Columbar/Colombard   VARIETY

Once important in France, mainly in Cognac, Columbar has fallen into relative disfavour. It gained importance in California – where it is called French Colombard – as the basis of jug wines (e.g. "California chablis"), but is being knocked out of the running by *Chardonnay*. A useful blending grape, it is mainly distilled into brandy, cognac or armagnac. A little can also be found in South Africa.

Descriptors Full coloured with good acidity, body and alcohol. Crisp and fruity with aromas of peach, nectarine and lemon. Can be tart and is not usually oaked. A reliable everyday wine that is best consumed young.

Food Matches Antipasto, melon, Parma ham, white fish, salads, Thai dishes.

■ Condrieu (con-dree-yuh)   APPELLATION

The Northern Rhône Valley in France produces this, one of the most fragrant wines, entirely from the low-yielding *Viognier* grape. It tends to be expensive due to its relative scarcity. Drink young, 1-3 years.

■ Cortese (di Gavi) (kor-TAY-zeh)   VARIETY

The top white grape of Piedmont, Italy, Cortese is a food-friendly wine that has been made in that region for well over a century. May appear as "Gavi" or as a varietal plus the regional name; Cortese de Gavi is the best known example. Not as plentiful as it once was, perhaps because of its somewhat neutral nature. Still, it is a very good food wine and pairs well with fish, although it can be pricey. Also found in Lombardy. (Cortese means "courteous".)

Descriptors Delicate, fruity aromas and flavours including lime, green gage and mineral, with good body and a tangy
26 citrus finish. May be treated to oak and malolactic to good

effect. High quality but not complex, and short lived.

Food Matches   Try with fish, seafoods, mushroom risotto, creamy pasta, oysters, charcuterie, pasta primavera, white truffles.

■ **Edelswicker** (AY-dl-zwih-ker)   STYLE

Literally "noble mixture", the term is used in France's Alsace region for a certain style of blended wine. Component grapes can include any of *Gewurztraminer, Auxerrois, Riesling, Pinot Gris, Muscat, Muscat Ottonel, Pinot Blanc,* and *Sylvaner* as well as *Chasselas, Pinot Noir* and *Pinot Meunier*. The wines are typically low-end, but can be made to a high quality. Generally soft and neutral with modest aromas.

■ **Ehrenfelser** (AIR-en-FELL-zer)   VARIETY

A German cross of *Riesling* and *Sylvaner,* dating from 1929, this is one of the better "neo-Riesling" grapes. Found principally in Germany's Pfalz and Rheinhessen, it often loses out to *Kerner,* although Ehrenfelser is considered the better grape. Important today in Canada's Okanagan valley.

Descriptors   At its best, much like Riesling, although with lower acid and less ageing ability.

Food Matches   SEE RIESLING.

■ **Elbling**   VARIETY

Widely planted in Roman times, mainly in Germany, Elbling is also found in Switzerland, Alsace, and Luxembourg. Quickly abandoned when better varieties became available, it is now mainly used in Sekt, a sparkling wine.

Descriptors   Light, somewhat neutral, suggesting apricots, with low alcohol and high acidity.

■ **Entre-deux-Mers** (on-truh doo mare)   APPELLATION

This subregion of Bordeaux, bounded by the Garonne and Gironde rivers, produces a blend from *Sauvignon Blanc, Semillon* and *Muscadelle*. The result is Sauvignon Blanc-like with a pleasant *Muscat* accent. Not overly exciting but reliable and usually good value.

Descriptors/Food Matches   SEE SAUVIGNON BLANC.

■ **Essensia**   STYLE

SEE TOKAJI.

■ **Fendant** (fawn-dawn)   VARIETY
See Chasselas.

■ **Folle Blanche/Gros Plant/Picpoul**   VARIETY
Although ordinary and almost characterless, Folle Blanche is
heavily used as a base wine to produce distilled wine products
including Cognac and Armagnac, and at one time went into
vermouth in Languedoc. It has the distinction of being one of
the parents of *Baco Noir*. Otherwise, acidic, neutral and uninteresting. Can also be found in California and Argentina.

■ **Fumé Blanc** (foo-may blahnk)   STYLE
An Americanisation of the Blanc Fumé of France's Pouilly
region, made popular by Robert Mondavi. Typically a full-
bodied *Sauvignon Blanc,* or sometimes *Semillon,* usually
with some oak treatment.

■ **Furmint** (foor-mint)   VARIETY
An important grape in Hungary where it produces a substantial varietal wine, Furmint is also an essential component
of *Tokaji* as it readily succumbs to Noble Rot. Rarely found
elsewhere, although there are limited plantings in Croatia,
Austria and South Africa. Less aromatic than *Harslevelü*, its
main blending partner, it responds well to ageing.
Descriptors   Produces a high-alcohol wine with abundant
extract, prominent acidity and complex, steely flavours suggesting apple, smoke, lime peel and pear.
Food Matches   Goulash, curry, poultry.

■ **Garganega** (gar-guh-NAY-guh)   VARIETY
Possibly originating in Hungary, this is the grape behind many
of Northern Italy's ubiquitous, bland white wines, especially in
Veneto. Often blended with the equally innocuous *Trebbiano,*
principally in Soave. On its own, Garganega can produce light
wines with decent character. Also found in Friuli and Umbria
where it has a lower profile. Can actually be improved by the
addition of *Trebbiano*.
Descriptors   Subtle, delicate and fresh with aromas of green
apples, citrus and almonds. Surprisingly age-worthy.
Food Matches   A light, food-friendly quaffer that goes well
with bruschetta, salad, gazpacho, pesto, prawns, and risotto.

■ **Gavi** (GAH-vee)   **APPELLATION**
SEE CORTESE.

■ **Geisenheim** (GUY-zen-HIME)   **HYBRID**
A cross of *Riesling* and *Chancellor,* the grape makes Riesling-like table wines often in a Germanic, i.e. off-dry, style, and occasionally Icewine. It is becoming popular in cool and cold climate regions, especially Ontario.
Descriptors The nose often shows pineapple, citrus, lime, and pepper.
Food Matches SEE RIESLING.

■ **Gewurztraminer** (geh-VERTS-truh-mee-ner)   **VARIETY**
One of the most distinctive of the noble grapes, "Gewurz" is for many an acquired taste. The name derives from the town of Tramin in north-eastern Italy, with the addition of the German word gewürz, which means "spicy". Alsace is the epicentre for dry Gewurztraminer, although the grape does extremely well elsewhere, especially Germany – where the wines are typically off-dry – and Niagara in Canada. Usually big, with over-the-top aromas, and in styles ranging from dry to late harvest and Icewines. Most table versions should be opened within 3 years of vintage.
Descriptors Deep gold, sometimes copper coloured, with lots of extract and soft acidity. Aromas include spice, rose petals, mango, lychee, and musk. At its best the palate shows lots of heft with an oily texture.
Food Matches BBQ chicken, calamari, grilled red peppers, curried beef or chicken, duck, paté, pork with sauerkraut, prosciutto, Roquefort, salami, Szechwan, smoked salmon, soft cheeses, sushi, Thai, veal, chicken paprikesh.
Late Harvest Foie gras, paté, puddings, fruit salsa, munster, gorgonzola, squash soup.

■ **Graubürgunder** (GRAOW-ber-gun-der)   **VARIETY**
The same grape as *Pinot Gris,* this German interpretation denotes a dryer, crisper style than *Ruländer.* Literally "grey burgundy".

■ **Grenache Blanc** (gruh-nosh blahN)   VARIETY

An important grape in the southern reaches of France, principally Languedoc and Rousillon, this varient of the red Grenache grape likely migrated from Spain, where it is called Garnacha Blanca. Often blended and sometimes oaked, it may appear as a varietal and can occasionally show up in red Rhône blends. Plantings are limited.

Descriptors   Rather pale with aromas of pear and anise. Good body and low acid. An early-drinking "picnic" wine that is best before its first birthday.

■ **Grüner-Veltliner** (GROO-ner FELT-lee-ner)   VARIETY

The number one white grape in Austria, its land of origin, "Gru Vee" has migrated only a little to other parts of Europe, including Hungary and the Czech Republic. Ranges from light to full bodied, sparkling and late harvest wines. Usually consumed young, it can age for up to 5 years or more. Interest in this grape is increasing world-wide.

Descriptors   Light to medium bodied, though it can be substantial. Crisp with a peppery, spicy, fruity nose. Mainly dry, sometimes with a light prickle.

Food Matches   Can be a good match for game, beef, poultry, veal, and pork. Excellent with schnitzel.

■ **Gütedel** (goo-teh-dell)   VARIETY

The same grape as *Chasselas* and *Fendant,* Gütedel is a popular table grape that dates back to ancient Egypt. Now found mainly in Eastern Europe and Germany as a winegrape, it is one of the parents of *Müller-Thurgau.*

Descriptors   Light, with low acid and alcohol. Pleasant when young, though rather neutral.

■ **Hürslevel** (HARSH-leh-vel-loo)   VARIETY

This is one of the most noble grapes of Hungary, where for centuries it has helped to produce the luscious dessert wine *Tokaji Aszú.* Prone to Noble rot, the grape accounts for up to 75% of the Tokaji blend. A little is also found in Slovakia and South Africa, though with less vinous success. Sometimes appears as a dry varietal wine as well as late harvest.

Descriptors   Table wines are aromatic, flowery, perfumy and spicy, with full body and deep colour.

■ **Huxelrebe** (hook-sell-RAY-beh)   VARIETY

A heavy-bearing grape popular in Germany and England, this cross of *Chasselas* and "Courtillier Musqué" was patented in 1927. Often blended, it otherwise produces a modest, aromatic wine with a *Muscat*-like character.

Descriptors Early drinking, fruity, flowery and racy, with Muscat perfume. Also good in a late harvest style.

■ **Irsai Olivér/Irsay Oliver** (EER-sigh olive-air)   VARIETY

A lively, aromatic grape peculiar to Hungary and Slovakia that dates from the 1930s, originally as a table grape. Produces a cheery-yet-serious aromatic wine the likes of *Muscat,* although it is considered to be a lesser grape. Usually offers good value.

Descriptors Light, often a bit sweet, with a Muscat-like nose, medium body and moderate acidity.

Food Matches SEE MUSCAT.

■ **Italian Riesling/Riesling Italico**   VARIETY

Considered to be an inferior clone of *Riesling,* the grape can be found in Northern Italy, principally Friuli and Veneto, and Eastern Europe as well as California and Canada. It can produce wines of good character but never as noble as the original. Called Olaszriesling in Hungary, "Italian Riesling" is the same grape as *Welchriesling.* (Most regions prohibit labelling the wine simply as "Riesling".)

■ **Jacquére** (zhah-care)   VARIETY

Peculiar to the Savoie region in the French Alps, Jacquére produces fresh, floral, fruity, nutty wines with a tendency to oxidize. Drink young.

■ Kerner   VARIETY

A relative newcomer, making its first appearance as recently as 1969, Kerner is a German cross of *Trollinger* (a red grape) and *Riesling*. Easy to grow and very forgiving of site selection, it often appears as a varietal, especially in the Franken, Baden, Rhinehessen and Pfalz regions, with few plantings outside of Germany. Can be found in *Liebfraumilch* blends. One of the few wines to still appear in a Bocksbeutal, it is very food friendly.

Descriptors   Similar to Riesling but less elegant, although it can display a high degree of quality. Hearty and fresh, with rich extract and a somewhat leafy quality. Can age well.

Food Matches   Asian dishes, blue cheese.

■ Klevner/Clevner   VARIETY

SEE PINOT BLANC.

■ Liebfraumilch (LEEB-fraow-milk)   STYLE

A popular blend that is, in fact, a higher quality wine than public opinion suggests. Usually made from *Müller-Thurgau, Silvaner* and *Kerner,* but may also contain *Riesling* and other grapes. (From "Die beruhmte Lieben Frauen Milch der Worms").

Descriptors   Mild, slightly sweet and appealing, but relatively bland; regulations specify it must be "pleasant".

Food Matches   Egg curry, fried chicken, Asian dishes, blue cheese.

■ Loureiro (loh-RAY-roh)   VARIETY

Named for the Laurel (bay) leaf, which its aroma sometimes resembles, Loureiro is essential in Portugal's Vinho Verde, and may appear there as a high quality varietal. Can also be found in Rias Baixas in Spain, where it produces a wine similar to Vinho Verde.

Descriptors   Aromas of spice, citrus and passionfruit; medium to full bodied, with good length and an "exciting" acidity.

Food Matches   Turkey salad. ALSO SEE VINHO VERDE.

■ Macabeo/Maccabéo (ma-kuh-BAY-oh)   VARIETY

One of Northern Spain's workhorse grapes, Macabeo is important in white Rioja and Cava. Often blended with *Bourboulenc* and Grenache Blanc in France. In Rioja, where it is called Viura, it may be used to soften red Rioja. Also found in Languedoc-Rousillon and North Africa.

Descriptors Capable of producing a quality, early-drinking wine with subtle fruit and floral aromas and low acid, but is more often light and neutral.

■ Madeleine Angevine   HYBRID

This early ripening grape is popular in Great Britain where it produces a palatable wine reminiscent of *Riesling,* with aromas of grass, citrus, melon and pear, and a bright acidity. Also used as a table grape.

■ Malvasia (mahl-vuh-SEE-uh)   VARIETY

Actually not one but several closely related grapes, both red and white, that originated in Greece more than 2000 years ago, and have since migrated to Italy, France, Spain, Portugal, and California. While sometimes seen carrying a varietal label, Malvasia is best known for its role in Madeira (which is called Malmsey in a purely British interpretation). Can be found blended with *Viura* in Spain and with *Trebbiano* in Italy, and even finds its way into red *Chianti.* Also the base of Tuscany's *Vin Santo* dessert wines.

Descriptors Produces a sweetish, substantial wine with light peach, apricot and nutty aromas and a tangy acidity. Table wines are best within two years of vintage.

■ Marsanne (marr-san/marr-zan)   VARIETY

Traditionally partnered with *Roussanne,* Marsanne goes into Hermitage Blanc and Crozes-Hermitage wines in France's Northern Rhône (where it is now becoming the more important part of the blend), and Côtes du Rhône Blanc. It may also appear in Hermitage red, and is emerging as a varietal wine in France's Midi. In Switzerland it's used for an off-dry wine called Ermitage. A little can be found in Australia and California.

Descriptors Rich and fragrant with aromas of citrus, peach, quince, jasmine, mineral, almond, and occasionally glue. Full-bodied, somewhat dark, with an oily texture. Can age well – up to 10 years – though most is best consumed young.

Food Matches Curry, tomato dishes, white fish, cream sauces, coconut dishes.

■ Melon de Bourgogne   VARIETY
(meh-lohN de boor-goh-nyuh)

A speciality of the Loire River Valley, the grape is more commonly known as *Muscadet,* and this is the only region that still uses it. Although it was at one time Burgundian, it was evicted from that region in the middle ages. Typically a light, simple wine that is often aged sur lie, resulting in a slight prickle, and may take light oak. A refreshing summer drink or aperitif, and just as often an undistinguished "jug wine", although the best can be quite substantial. Muscadet is now accepted as a varietal name. Drink in its first year. (Some of the *"Pinot Blanc"* in California is actually Melon.)

Descriptors   Dry, crisp, light,and somewhat neutral, with creamy softness, crisp acidity, often with a light tingle.

Food Matches   One of the best shellfish wines around, especially with fresh mussels and scallops. Also salads, antipasti, veal, egg dishes, clams, crayfish, crudité, grilled veg, fruit-based salads, grilled shrimp, mild fish, oysters, sole, jellied eel, gravad lox.

■ Morio Muscat   VARIETY
A cross between *Sylvaner* and *Wiessburgunder* – and therefore not a true Muscat grape – Morio Muscat is planted extensively in Germany, where it was for a time the backbone of *Liebfraumilch.* Now mainly used for blending with *Silvaner,* it is falling out of favour, although it can often be found as a nicely priced varietal.

Descriptors   Highly perfumed – similar to Muscat – with grape, musk and grapefruit aromas, medium body and good acidity.

Food Matches   SEE MUSCAT.

■ Moscatel de Sétubel (shtoo-bl)   APPELLATION
This sweet fortified wine is produced in Southern Portugal from the *Muscat of Alexandria* grape.

■ Moscato Bianco/Moscato di Canelli   VARIETY
The main Muscat grape of Italy. (SEE MUSCAT BLANC.)

■ **Moscofilero** (MOSS-koh-FEE-lair-roh)   VARIETY
This pink-skinned grape is popular in Southern Greece, where it produces wine valued for its aromatic floral notes, spiciness, and crisp *Muscat*-like character.

■ **Müller-Thurgau** (MOO-lair TOOR-gaow)   VARIETY
A European cross created by Hermann Müller, a native of the canton of Thurgau in Switzerland. Once thought to have been developed from *Sylvaner* and *Riesling,* it is more likely a *Chasselas/Riesling* cross. Widely planted in Europe and some parts of the New World, especially New Zealand, Great Britain, Oregon and Washington. Good if not over-cropped, otherwise it leans toward dull, flabby and "mousy", although late harvest styles can be quite good. It lacks ageing potential and may yet lose out to more promising varieties. Best examples are from Germany's Reinhessen, Pfalz and Mosel.
Descriptors   At its best, somewhat similar to Riesling, showing floral, sometimes grapey aromas and a light acidity. Soft, round and light bodied, it can as often be dull and short on acid, with a neutral nose.
Food Matches   SEE RIESLING.

■ **Muscadelle**   VARIETY
One of the most plentiful white grapes in Bordeaux, Muscadelle rarely appears on its own and is used instead to add aroma to *Entre-deux-Mers,* as well as Bordeaux Blanc and *Sauternes,* partnering with *Semillon* and *Sauvignon Blanc*. Although somewhat grapey and similar to *Muscat,* it does not appear to be related. Used in Australia in their "Tokay", a dark, rich, fortified dessert wine. Some limited plantings exist in California, though it is being used there less and less.
Descriptors   Fragrant, grapey, with Muscat-like aromas and medium body.

■ **Muscadet** (moos-cuh-day)   APPELLATION/VARIETY
This regional name is now accepted as a variety name for *Melon de Bourgogne* in the Muscadet region of the Loire Valley.

■ **Muscadine**   VARIETY

This North American family of grapes includes the Rondiflora
and *Scuppernong* varieties. Found throughout the south-
eastern US, its members produce lighter wines that show
mainly grapey and musty character, light colour – neither red
nor white – and often sweet.

■ **Muscat (Blanc à Petite Grains)**   VARIETY

One of the oldest known varieties and grown virtually everywhere, Muscat can range from dry to very sweet, subtle to
overpowering. Found in Asti Spumante and the fortified dessert wine "Tokay" from Australia, it is one of the few Vinifera
grapes that yields a "grapey" wine. Also popular as a table
grape. Often a bargain and ideal in warm weather. (Not related to *Muscadelle, Muscadet* or *Muscadine*.)

Descriptors   Low acid, fragrant and fruity, with aromas of
peach, apple, honey, roses, and Muscat grapes. Can also be
pungent, musky or piney, and can be slightly bitter. Usually
dry to medium-dry, and refreshing.

Food Matches   Dry/Off-dry: Avocado salad, chicken with
grapes, curried beef or chicken, spicy seafoods, mascarpone,
ginger, saté, tabouleh, quiche, hummus.

Sweeter Styles: Chocolate, mince pie, sorbet, puddings, fruit
salad, munster, tapenade, nuts, stir-fried chicken.

■ **Muscat d'Alsace** (m. dahl-sass)   VARIETY

A close relative of *Muscadelle* (although some claim it is just
Muscat Blanc), Muscat d'Alsace produces a grapey, usually dry
wine comparable to a *Riesling/Gewurztraminer* blend.

■ **Muscat of Alexandria**   VARIETY

This ancient grape, possibly originating in Egypt, is now
found in most grape growing regions. Its main use is in Portugal's fortified *Moscatel de Setubel* and Italy's *Zibibbo,* and
occasionally as a dry wine in South Africa. Otherwise, much
of the production ends up at the distillery, in the fruit bowl or
as packets of raisins.

■ **Muscat Ottonel**   VARIETY

A cross of *Chasselas* and a lesser *Muscat,* Ottonel is the least
distinctive of the Muscat family of grapes, showing less of
everything. Still, it makes a respectable Muscat-style wine

principally in Hungary, Romania, Alsace, the Ukraine, and lesser-known areas of Eastern Europe. Apparently good with smoked herring.

■ New York Muscat   HYBRID

A cross between Muscat Hamburg and "Ontario" (a *Labrusca* grape) that was introduced to the North-eastern US in 1961, this very productive grape is often made into off-dry to sweet Muscat-like wines, or used to add perfume to blends.

■ Niagara   VARIETY

Important at one time in North America's eastern wine regions, especially Ontario and New York State, Niagara is essentially a white version of *Concord*. It produces a serviceable wine with a typically grapey (foxy) profile, and is now mainly used for preserves and juice. A cross of Concord and Cassady.

■ Optima   VARIETY

A newer vinifera cross, dating from 1971, whose parents include "Sylvaner x Riesling" and *Müller-Thurgau*. Although often lacking in character, it is used in the Mosel and Rheinhessen to add some substance to their vin ordinaire. Also important in Austria, its main selling point is that it ripens reliably in cool climates. Well suited to late harvest styles, but is falling into disuse.

Descriptors   Optima tends to produce "blowsy" wines (i.e. somewhat dull with high alcohol).

■ Orange Muscat   VARIETY

This sub-species of *Muscat* has a distinct aroma of oranges, and is grown exclusively in California where it is the basis of branded dessert wines.

■ Ortega   VARIETY

Hailing from Germany, this cross of *Müller-Thurgau* and *Siegerrebe* is found only in its homeland, where it's used to add aroma to *Riesling* in lesser years, and also in parts of Canada. Although the grapes ripens with high levels of sugar, they often lack adequate acidity.

■ Palomino (PAL-oh-MEE-noh)   VARIETY

The most important grape in Jerez, Spain, Palomino is used to produce dryer style sherries. Sometimes appears as a table wine, though it appears to be ill-suited to that task as it oxidizes easily. Also found in Australia, California, France, and South Africa. (ALSO SEE PEDRO XIMÉNEZ.)

Descriptors Palomino-based sherries are pale, dry and refined.

■ Parrellada   VARIETY

Found throughout Spain, the grape is important in the production of Cava. It can produce quality aromatic and refreshing table wines that benefit from barrel time and can age well, though it is as often low in character, suitable only for blending.

■ Pedro Ximénez (PEH-droh HEE-MAN-nez)   VARIETY

Affectionately known as PX, this is the grape that gives us sweet sherry. Grown throughout Spain's Jerez region, it is also found in Australia where it is used to produce dry, slightly neutral white and late harvest wines. Also found to a lesser degree in Argentina, South Africa and California. Now less important than *Palomino* in sherry production.

Descriptors Produces sweet sherries that are rich and tangy with a distinctive burnt note.

■ Picpoul (pick-pool)   VARIETY

SEE FOLLE BLANCHE.

■ Pinot Blanc/Bianco (pee-noh blahN/bee-YON-koh)
                                                 VARIETY

A mutated strain of Pinot Gris, the grape evolved more than a century ago and was quickly recognized for its potential. Found throughout Europe and the New World, it is especially prominent in Alsace. Also very popular in Germany and Austria, and now making in-roads in California as well as Canada's Niagara and BC wine regions. Sometimes mistaken for *Chardonnay,* especially when young, it fares well in oak barriques yet can produce excellent un-oaked wines. Sometimes made into a sparkling wine. (ALSO SEE WEISSBURGUNDER, KLEVNER.)

Descriptors Full bodied and less aromatic than Chardonnay
with a higher acidity. Aromas can include floral, apple and

almond. Spicy, fruity and rounded but not aggressive, it is usually better when young, though it will age for a few years.

Food Matches An excellent food wine and especially good with alfredo sauce, "brunch", veal, camembert, egg dishes, charcuterie, chévre, feta, hamburgers, pesto, paté, pork, shellfish, Thai green curry, turkey, sushi, risotto.

■ Pinot Gris/Grigio (pee-noh gree/GREEd-joh) VARIETY

Sometimes called "Tokay Pinot Gris" in Alsace, the grey pinot, a mutation of *Pinot Noir,* produces a medium to full bodied, low acid, aromatic wine. Rich, smokey and honeyed in Alsace, spicy in Oregon, and sweet in Germany, whereas Italian Pinot Grigio can be floral and honeyed or quite neutral. As German Grauburgunder it is often oaked. The current darling of the aromatic grapes, it is best from 1-6 years. Also known as R lander in Germany.

Descriptors Soft and perfumy with peach, orange rind, honey and spice aromas. Medium bodied, often copper coloured, usually crisp and refreshing. It can be intense.

Food Matches Mushrooms, ravioli, borscht, brie/camembert, chévre, BBQ or roast chicken, gnocchi, goose, fish stock, parmigiano, cream sauce, pasta, pork, smoked salmon, quiche, sushi.

■ Pouilly Fuisée (pwee-yee fwee-say) APPELLATION

This well-known sub-appellation of the Maconaisse produces a quality Burgundy from the *Chardonnay* grape.

■ Pouilly Fumé (pwee-yee foo-may) APPELLATION

Hailing from the Loire River valley in France, this wine is made entirely from the aromatic *Sauvignon Blanc* grape. It can be medium to full bodied, ranging from simple to complex, and is best within 3-4 years of vintage. Fumé refers to a smokey quality that comes from the soil. (ALSO SEE BLANC FUMÉ, FUMÉ BLANC.)

Descriptors Sometimes compared to a "Viognier-Sauvignon Blanc" blend, with pepper, wildflowers, mineral, a distinctive gunflint aroma, and a racy acidity.

Food Matches Try with lobster, shrimp, crab, oysters, bean dishes, brie/camembert, chévre, hollandaise, cream sauces, chicken, poached salmon, smoked salmon, veal.

■ **Prosecco** (proh-SEH-coh) **VARIETY**

Native to the Friuli region in Northern Italy, the Prosecco grape is overshadowed by the wine of the same name. Almost always a sparkling wine made using the Charmat method, Prosecco comes in two grades: Conegliano and the higher quality Valdobiadenne. Fun but never frivolous and often a bargain, Prosecco is an excellent aperitif or any-occasion sparkler. A little is grown in Argentina.

Descriptors Intensely aromatic, fruity, creamy, delicate and appley fresh. Dry, sometimes off-dry, often with a pleasant bitterness on the finish.

Food Matches Anywhere that Champagne would work and also great by itself.

■ **Reichensteiner** (Rye-ken-STY-ner) **VARIETY**

Introduced in the late 1930s, this grape is a cross of *Müller-Thurgau* and "Madeleine Angevine x Calabrese", taking its character mainly from the Müller-Thurgau, though less intense. Useful as a blending grape but also found as a varietal, mainly in England and Germany and, to a lesser degree, Italy and New Zealand.

■ **Retsina** **STYLE**

One of Greece's most popular wines for nearly 3,000 years, with a distinctive aroma that originally came from the pine resin used to seal ancient containers. Made mostly from the *Savatiano* grape, retsina is still flavoured with pine resin.

■ **Rotitis/Rhoditis** (roh-DEE-teez) **VARIETY**

Found in parts of Greece and Macedonia, this indigenous pinkish grape can show a range of skin colours, attributed to a proliferation of clones in the vineyard. The wines are light and fruity with a fresh acidity.

■ **Rieslaner** (REEZ-lan-er) **VARIETY**

A cross of *Sylvaner* and *Riesling,* developed around 1921 at the Wurzberg Institute in Germany, Rieslaner produces a wine similar to Riesling though of less over-all quality. It has good balance with some ageing ability, and in the right hands it can produce near-Riesling character.

Descriptors Rich extract, somewhat neutral, with currant aromas and a racy acidity.

40 ***Food Matches*** SEE RIESLING.

■ Riesling (REEZ-ling/REECE-ling)   VARIETY

Often called the "queen" of the noble grapes, Riesling is one of about a half-dozen truly exceptional white grapes and is grown nearly everywhere, although it prefers cool climates. Light to medium bodied, it is almost never oaked. A versatile and usually good value wine, it can be found as dry, off-dry, semi-sweet, late harvest, Icewine, and Trockenbeerenauslese, and is one of the grapes that can become the delightful German sparkling wine called Sekt. Quality Riesling can age for up to 30 years, and is good from 2 years on. Sometimes called Johannesbeg Riesling. (The name has often been borrowed and attached to a number of less worthy grapes.)

Descriptors   Aromas can range from fruity, flowery, apple, honey, lime, peaches and slate, all the way to paraffin, petrol and coal oil. Fresh, sometimes lean and often made in a sweeter style, it can be low in alcohol (7-9%) with no diminution of character or ageability.

Food Matches   Asian foods, chévre, avocado salad, chicken stir fry, crab, curried beef, Danish blue, emmentaler, foie gras, poached sole, liver, lobster newburg, munster, pork with sauerkraut, roast goose or duck, roasted vegetables, roquefort, scallops, shellfish, camembert, smoked salmon, sweet & sour pork, turkey.

Late Harvest, Icewine, TBA: Apple or raspberry pudding, gorgonzola, foie gras.

■ Roussanne (roo-san)   VARIETY

One of only two grapes allowed in white Hermitage (the other being *Marsanne*) in the Northern Rhône, as well as in Châtauneuf-du-Pape and Rhône whites. Also found in Languedoc-Rousillon, but is little known outside of France. Modest plantings can be found in Tuscany and Australia. Losing ground to Marsanne.

Descriptors   Light bodied, elegant and aromatic with an herbal nose showing pear, floral and mineral notes, and moderate acidity. Can be oaked and is age worthy.

Food Matches   Curry, ocean fish, cream sauces.

■ **Rousette (de Savoie)** (roo-set de sa-vwah)   **VARIETY**

Of mainly historical interest, this grape is very similar to *Furmint* in character and is found mainly in North-eastern France, principally Savoie and Bugey. Look for "Rousette de Savoie" on the label. A highly perfumed, quality wine with herbal, lemon and mineral aromas and good acidity, it will last a few years after vintage.

■ **Ruländer** (roo-lan-der)   **VARIETY**

A German synonym for *Pinot Gris* that is sometimes used to indicate a sweeter style of wine (See Graubürgunder).

Descriptors Light to medium bodied with aromas of honey, spice, earth, and mushroom.

■ **Sancerre** (san-sair)   **APPELLATION**

This, one of the best known "racy" white wines, is made in the Upper Loire River valley near the town of Sancerre entirely from *Sauvignon Blanc* grapes. Usually lighter and more refreshing than Pouilly-Fumé, Sancerre can be an outstanding and distinctive wine, and is especially good in summer weather. Best at 3-4 years. (Note that red Sancerre is *Pinot Noir*.)

Descriptors Known for its spicy, green grass and mineral aromas and racy acidity.

Food Matches Shellfish, delicate fish, rainbow trout, chévre, brie.

■ **Sauternes** (saw-tairn)   **APPELLATION**

Considered by many to be the greatest of the dessert wines, Sauternes is produced in the Sauternes region of Bordeaux from botrytized *Semillon, Sauvignon Blanc* and *Muscadelle* grapes. Sauternes' price is pushed ever upward because of the many passes the pickers must make through the vineyards to harvest only grapes which are ready. Barsac, a sub-region of Sauternes, produces a near-identical wine that shows nearly as much quality. Sauternes is legendary for ageing – 50 to 100 years and more. (Some New World regions for a time marketed white jug wines as "sauterne" or "dry sauterne".)

Descriptors Rich and elegant, with stone fruit, tropical fruit and honey flavours, a viscous texture and a firm acidity. The deep golden colour deepens over the years.

Food Matches While the sauternais will pair the wine with every course of a meal, Roquefort and foie gras are its traditional companions.

■ **Sauvignon Blanc** (soh-vee-nyon blahN)   VARIETY

The "savage" grape can produce good to exceptional wines in just about any soil, and always shows its distinctive character, especially in New Zealand. The grape behind *Sancerre*, Bordeaux Blanc, Pouilly Fumé and, in California, *Fumé Blanc*, it is sometimes blended with *Semillon* and is occasionally oaked. Can also be found as Late Harvest or TBA styles. An easy match with lighter foods.

Descriptors   Mostly medium bodied, with herbaceous, grassy, grapefruit, gooseberry, passionfruit, mineral, asparagus, and nettle aromas – and occasionally tom cat or "pipi du chat" – always with a crisp, robust acidity.

Food Matches   Asparagus quiche, brie/camembert, Thai food, fish with dill, green salads, grilled peppers, havarti, herbed or grilled chicken or pork, salmon/trout, hollandaise sauce, Monterey jack, shellfish, chévre, shrimp, spring rolls, tomato dishes, tuna, vegetarian dishes, chicken teriyaki, tostados.

■ **Savatiano** (sa-va-tee-a-noh)   VARIETY

An important grape in Greece used mainly to produce *Retsina*, a resinated wine, Savatiano can also produce decent table wines with citrus and floral character, although somewhat low in acidity.

■ **Schönburger** (SHOWN-ber-ger)   VARIETY

Introduced in 1979, this pink-skinned vinifera grape produces fruity, spicy wines with low acidity and good body, similar to *Muscat* and sometimes *Gewurztraminer*. Originally from Germany, it is now found mainly in Great Britain.

■ **Scuppernong**   VARIETY

A candidate for the most amusing name, Scuppernong is an ancient Muscadine grape, native to the south-eastern United States, that enjoyed its greatest popularity during the American Revolution, but is now mainly a curiosity.

■ **Sémillon** (seh-mee-yoN)   **VARIETY**

Grown extensively in France's Graves region, Australia and California, Semillon can produce a top quality wine, similar to *Sauvignon Blanc,* although it can be somewhat plain when young. Will age typically 2-6 years and even up to 10. Sometimes it is blended with *Chardonnay* or *Sauvignon Blanc* – a popular trick in Australia – and may be oaked. Australia also produces a robust varietal. The grape is a major part of *Sauternes* as it readily succumbs to noble rot. (Also see Fumé Blanc.)

Descriptors Lemon, gooseberry, fresh figs, grass, and nectarines, with good body and soft acidity. Can be nutty, honeyed and rich, with a silky lanolin texture when well aged.

Food Matches Fish in rich sauces, honey-roasted or BBQ poultry, mussels, prawns, oysters, swordfish, roast beef, spicy pork, roast turkey, haddock, chicken kebobs.

Late Harvest: Fontina, friulano, cheddar, roquefort, cream-based puddings.

■ **Seyval Blanc/Seyve Villard**   **HYBRID**

Seyval is an important French hybrid grape that enjoys a strong following in the cool, sometimes unreliable climates of Eastern North America, especially New York State and Niagara, as well as Great Britain. Not at all foxy, the wine is sometimes compared to *Chardonnay,* but lacks that grape's sophistication. It readily takes to both malolactic fermentation and oak finishing. Now banned from mainland European vineyards.

Descriptors Light and fresh with aromas of green plum, flowers, grass, nettles, and herbs, though sometimes nondescript. Best when young, it can develop a nutty depth after a few years of ageing.

Food Matches Brie, cheddar, havarti, mussels, salads, clams, poached fish, sole, bass, olives, pork, poultry, roasted peppers, vegetarian dishes.

■ **Scheurebe** (shoy-RAY-beh)   **VARIETY**

This relatively rare grape is important in Germany and is also found in Austria. Named after vine breeder Dr. Georg Scheu, it is a cross of *Sylvaner* and *Riesling,* and first appeared in the early 1900s. Capable of producing top quality wines similar to *Riesling,* it is valued for its ability to produce "auslessen" (sweet wines) sometimes from nobly-rotted grapes. Suitable for ageing, it is also found as a late harvest style as well as Eiswein.

Descriptors Spicy, floral, slightly grapey, it may also display blackcurrant and grapefruit aroma and flavour, with good body and a "nervy" acidity.

Food Matches SEE RIESLING.

■ Siegerrebe (SEE-ger-RAY-beh)   VARIETY

A newer grape variety limited to Germany that shows a "ponderous" *Gewurztraminer*-like character. Often made in a late harvest style as its sugar levels tend to be quite high. Otherwise mainly useful as a blending grape.

■ Silvaner/Sylvaner   VARIETY

Sometimes called the poor man's *Riesling,* Sylvaner is a well established grape that has been grown since medieval times. Originally from Germany, it is now found in Austria, Northern Italy and Eastern Europe, but it appears to be losing ground to *Müller-Thurgau,* a less interesting grape. In Franken, however, it continues to produce characterful, food-friendly wines, usually appearing in a Bocksbeutel. Almost unknown in New World vineyards.

Descriptors Sylvaner produces a graceful, delicate, racy, albeit somewhat neutral wine. Sometimes made off-dry or even sweet. A useful quaffing wine and very food friendly, with some ageing ability.

Food Matches Poached fish, anchovies, mild cheese, poultry, sweet & sour sauces, quiche, sweetbreads, seafoods, timbales, lighter meats.

■ Soave (swah-veh)   APPELLATION

This light, acidic wine from Veneto in Italy is made mainly from the *Trebbiano* and *Garganega* grapes. With a good chill, it makes the perfect picnic wine, although its main advantage is that it is cheap and plentiful. Estate bottlings can be quite good.

Descriptors Slightly fruity, fairly simple, with aromas of lemon and almond, mild flavours and a racy acidity. Often shows a touch of bitter almond on the finish.

Food Matches Pasta, canapés, poached fish, lunch.

■ Steen

VARIETY

A name given to *Chenin Blanc* in South Africa that is disappearing from labels in favour of the grape's proper name.

■ Symphony

HYBRID

A newer hybrid developed at the University of California at Davis by crossing "Grüner Veltliner x Gewürztraminer" with *Muscat of Alexandria*. Somewhat spicy, with aromas of peach and apricot, it bears a resemblance to *Malvasia* or *Riesling,* and can be found as dry to off-dry wines and sometimes sparklers.

■ Tocai Friulano (toe-KYE)

VARIETY

Not to be confused with "Tokay" (*Pinot Gris*) of Alsace or *Tokaji* of Hungary, this distinctively Italian grape produces fresh, young white wines in the Friuli region. Almost unknown outside of Italy, although there are isolated plantings in Chile, where it is sometimes called Sauvignon Vert. The grape may be a relative of Hungary's *Furmint*. (The name "Tocai" was outlawed in 2006, the EU having given title preference to Hungary's Tokaji.)

Descriptors Usually a good quality, every day white wine for early consumption. Fresh, crisp and light bodied with floral and almond aromas and a somewhat oily texture.

Food Matches A versatile food wine and an ideal accompaniment to lighter fish.

■ Tokaji (Aszú) (toe-KYE a-SOO)

APPELLATION

This venerable Hungarian dessert wine is made primarily from desiccated *Furmint* grapes along with *Hárslevelü* and Yellow Muscat. A mash of nobly-rotted grapes is added to a base wine and the result is aged for years in mouldy cellars. Sweetness is rated in "Putts", short for puttonyos, which is approximately 1 bushel of botrytis-affected mash. Thus a "3 putts" wine would have 3 baskets of dried grapes added to the must, and it can go as dense as 6 putts. Intensely sweet, comparable to *Sauternes* or *Icewine,* and often a very good bargain. Essensia is the name given to a similar wine made wholey from nobly-rotted grapes.

Descriptors Intense honey, musk, hay, barley sugar, marzipan, and garrigue aromas, with a highly viscous texture.

Exceptional ageability – up to a century or more.

Food Matches Gorgonzola, orange mousse, foie gras, black truffles, carrot cake, Christmas pudding, Thai foods.

■ Torrontés (tor-ron-tayz)   VARIETY

Originating in Galicia, Cordoba and other parts of Spain, Torrontés is finding a second home in Argentina. Also found in Rioja, Ribera del Duero and Chile, it's mainly used as a blending grape although it can appear as an attractive varietal.

Descriptors Light, early drinking, with high acidity and *Muscat*-like aromas.

■ Traminer (TRA-min-er)   VARIETY

The direct ancestor of *Gewurztraminer,* Traminer is almost identical though with a lighter skin and less aroma. It is common in Eastern Europe and Italy's Alto Adige, where you will find the town of Tramin, which gives the grape its name. The name is sometimes used as a synonym for Gewurztraminer.

Descriptors SEE GEWURZTRAMINER.

■ Traminette   HYBRID

Developed at Cornell University and introduced in 1996, this cross of *Seyval Blanc* and *Gewurztraminer* can be found mainly in New York's Finger Lakes and Niagara in Ontario. The wine is spicy and fragrant with aromas of honey and apricot, a slightly bitter finish, and with good ageing potential.

■ Trebbiano (treh-byah-noh)   VARIETY

This widely planted grape has the distinction of being important yet little respected. Its main use is to produce oceans of neutral white table wines, especially in Italy, although it can show character if handled carefully. Rivals *Airen* for producing the "most" wine. As *Ugni Blanc,* it is the basis of many French brandies. In Italy, it can be found in Verdicchio, Orvieto, Frascati, Soave, *Vin Santo,* even *Chianti,* and also as a varietal. Now found in Portugal, Eastern Europe, Mexico, Argentina, South Africa, and Australia. Easy to cultivate and high yielding, it is routinely used as a blending grape to extend bulk wines.

Descriptors Relatively neutral, with subtle citrus and almond aromas. Usually crisp with low extract, it can be low in acid, verging on flabby.

Food Matches Schnitzel, spinach cannelloni, mussels, fried rice, veal, pork, stir fried chicken, jellied eels, polenta, pizza.   *47*

■ **Triomphe (d'Alsace)** (tree-omph doll-sass)   **HYBRID**
Found almost exclusively in Great Britain, this Kulhman cultivar is hardy and disease resistant, but suffers from foxy aromas.

■ **Ugni Blanc** (oon-yee blahN)   **VARIETY**
This is the name for *Trebbiano* in France, where it appears almost exclusively in brandy, cognac, and armagnac. May have been imported from Italy as far back as the 14th century and, despite a general lack of quality, it is one of France's most planted varieties.

■ **Verdejo** (ver-DAY-yoh)   **VARIETY**
Found in Rueda, Ribera del Duero and Castilla in Spain, Verdejo produces quality, long-lived table wines with character. Also important as a blending partner, and as the basis for a sherry-style wine made in Rueda. Now being challenged by *Sauvignon Blanc,* which it often resembles.
Descriptors   Aromatic with citrus, herbaceous and nutty aromas and good extract. Can age well.

■ **Verdelho/Verdello** (ver-DAY-yoh)   **VARIETY**
One of the grapes behind Portugal's madeira, but now falling into disuse there. In Australia, where it is pronounced ver-DELL-oh, it produces good quality, dry, varietally-named wines.
Descriptors   Rich, tangy lemon-lime flavours with good acidity. Australian examples can be substantial and interesting.
Food Matches   Indian curries, roast vegetables, roast chicken.

■ Verdicchio (vair-DIH-kee-oh)   VARIETY

Not a particularly exciting wine, yet somewhat underrated, Verdicchio is important to the Marche region in central Italy where it creates clean, crisp, almost colourless wines. Matelica and Castelli dei Jesi are the most reliable DOC regions. The wine of the same name is ubiquitous in Central Italy, where its distinctive amphora-shaped green bottle gives it away. Always light and fresh with sufficient character, it may also be oaked, sparkling or late harvest.

Descriptors   Light in body and colour, with subtle aromas of lemon and almond. Fresh, fruity, well structured and refreshing, slightly bitter and fairly high in acidity.

Food Matches   Smoked salmon, fish & chips, scallops, sushi, minestrone, marinara, veal scaloppini, avocado, schnitzel, eggs Florentine, seafood salad, linguine in cream sauce, pesto, antipasti.

■ Vermentino (VER-men-TEE-noh)   VARIETY

Found mainly in Liguria, Corsica and Sardinia, this Italian grape is similar to *Malvasia* but shows a livelier character. Called Malvoisie in Corsica, where it is the leading white grape. Often blended with *Trebbiano,* it can take a few years in the bottle.

Descriptors   Richly coloured with aromas of ripe apples, citrus and honey, good body and a lively acidity.

■ Vernaccia (di San Gimignano)   APPELLATION
(ver-NA-chee-yuh dee SAN jim-in-YAN-oh)

Since the 1300s, Vernaccia has been a staple on Tuscan dinner tables. The name itself suggests an everyday wine, i.e. "in the vernacular". Also found in Southern Italy as well as in Sardinian "sherry", it was once considered the greatest white wine of Italy, and it is very food friendly. May have originated in Greece.

Descriptors   Although somewhat elusive, the wines tend to be substantial, with deep colour, good body and a crisp acidity. Sometimes treated to oak.

Food Matches   Spinach ravioli, pasta, pesto, alfredo sauce, salmon, herb sauces, lasagne al forno, antipasti.

■ **Vidal (Blanc)/Vidal 256** (vee-dahl blahN)   HYBRID

This French Hybrid grape, a cross between "Siebel 4986" and *Ugni Blanc,* dates from the end of the 19th century. The grape can produce neutral plonk, but at its best is very much like *Sauvignon Blanc.* One of the most important grapes in Niagara, Ontario, where it is responsible for much of their *Icewine* and late harvest wines. Also grown in the Eastern US, it suffers mainly from the stigma of its North American parentage.

Descriptors   Lean, fruity, crisp and attractive every day wines smacking of citrus. Late harvest and Icewines are rich, unctuous, and laden with aromas of honey, stone fruits and mangoes. Can age very well, 5 years or more.

Food Matches   Lemon chicken, pork loin, shellfish, fresh water fish, salmon, lobster, crab, white fish, vegetarian dishes, turkey.

Late Harvest, Icewine: Lancashire, gorgonzola, roquefort, stilton, creme caramel.

■ **Vignoles** (vin-yole)   HYBRID

Introduced in the late 19th century, this hybrid grape is found throughout the north-eastern and middle US, particularly New York's Finger Lakes, as well as eastern Canada. It produces a well-balanced wine with high acidity and tropical fruit aromas, and is especially good as a late harvest wine.

■ **Vilana**   VARIETY

Limited to the Greek island of Crete, Vilana produces delicate, early-drinking wines.

■ **Viognier** (vee-oh-nyay)   VARIETY

Considered by some to be the ultimate white grape, Viognier is low yielding and temperamental to grow, and therefore somewhat rare. It is found in only a few of France's appellations, especially Condrieu in the Rhône. The wines are full bodied and low in acidity with intriguing aromas and flavours, and are gaining interest in the New World, principally Australia, Canada and Brazil. Best when consumed within 3 years of vintage.

Descriptors   Golden to slightly rosé, rich and elegant. Soft yet strong, with silky texture, high alcohol and a heady bouquet. Aromas can include May blossoms, apricots, musky peaches, and ripe pears.

Food Matches   Artichokes, BBQ or honey-mustard chicken, crab, lobster, shrimp, gazpacho, mild East Indian dishes, salads, scallops, whitefish, aged gouda, roast beef, pork.

■ Vinho Verde (VEEN-yoh VAIRD)   APPELLATION

In Portugal, verde means "green", as in a young wine, but also alludes to the verdant vineyards where these wines originate. Mainly a light bodied and slightly spritzy white wine, it is usually just off-dry but can be dry, sometimes with low alcohol. Made mostly from *Alvarinho* grapes, Vinho Verde is best within one year of vintage, and is good as an aperitif. There are also red and rosé versions of Vinho Verde, and the better ones are worth trying.

Descriptors   Aromas can include apple, apricot, lemon, peach, and mineral. Usually light but can be substantial, often with a light prickle from sitting on the lees.

Food Matches   Oily fish, sardines, salads, turkey, quiche, dirty rice, aubergine fritters.

■ Vin Santo/Vinsanto   APPELLATION

Most commonly a sweet dessert wine, this recioto wine is a speciality of Tuscany, and is made from partially dried *Trebbiano* and *Malvasia* grapes. The wines are fermented and stored in barrels for prolonged periods – up to eight years – and may undergo several fermentations, which results in considerable variability from producer to producer. Dry and off-dry versions are seen occasionally. Greece also produces a Vinsanto fortified wine from *Assyrtico* and "Aidani", a red grape. (The name means "holy wine".)

Descriptors   Deeply coloured, very sweet and viscous, with apricot, orange and nutty or sherry-like aromas.

Food Matches   Gorgonzola and biscotti are classic companions.

■ Viura (vee-yur-uh)   VARIETY

A local name for *Macabeo,* Viura is important in Spain and is the main white grape of Rioja. It shows a crisp acidity in either dry or off-dry, every day table wines. Often blended with *Malvasia.*

Descriptors   Light, fresh, appley.

■ **Vouvray** (voo-vray)   APPELLATION

This region in the Loire River Valley produces wines from 100% *Chenin Blanc*. Styles range from dry to quite sweet, even a sparklers, although the labels give the buyer little guidance as to which style is in the bottle. Can be vinted to a super-premium, rare and costly wine. Sweet versions can easily be aged for 20 years or more. Open lesser wines within 4 years.

Descriptors   The dry wines show a high, almost searing, acidity, with aromas of buttermilk, honey and ripe peaches, usually with good body.

Food Matches   White meats, ocean fish, white fish in beurre blanc.

■ **Welchriesling/Welch Riesling**   VARIETY

Not a *Riesling* grape but wide-spread and popular, especially in Austria, Hungary, parts of Eastern Europe, and even China. The same grape as Italian Riesling, it is unknown in France and Germany. The grape's origin is a mystery, and it is known by a variety of off-beat names.

Descriptors   Fresh, fruity, spicy and refreshing, with light body, although it can be bland. Drink young.

■ **Weissburgunder/Weisser Burgunder**   VARIETY
(VICE-berr-gun-der)

A name given to *Pinot Blanc* in Germany.

■ **Xarel-lo** (sah-REL-loh)   VARIETY

One of the component grapes of traditional Spanish Cava (along with *Parellada* and *Macabeo*) adding a somewhat vegetal note. Quite flavourful, but shows less overall quality than its blending partners.

■ **Zibibbo**   VARIETY

An uncommon variety of *Muscat of Alexandria* that is grown in Sicily. Mainly for use in sweet fortified wines and also as a table grape.

Notes

Notes

Notes

Red

Winegrapes

A-Z

■ **Aghiorghitiko** (a-yor-YEE-tee-koh) **VARIETY**
The "St. George" grape (named after the town of Agios Georgios, (now called Nemea) is the second most prolific red grape in Greece, where it makes soft, fruity, full-bodied and age-worthy wines. It can appear as a varietal as well as a rosé, and is often used for blending.
Food Matches SEE MERLOT.

■ **Aglianico** (al-YAHN-nee-koh) **VARIETY**
This deeply coloured, aromatic and intensely flavoured grape, likely dating from the 7th century, is important in Italy's Campania, Calabria and Apulia regions. Produces good red and rosé wines, although it can be coarse when young.
Descriptors Earthy, tarry, with subtle berry and chocolate aromas. Concentrated and long lasting, with high acid and tannin.
Food Matches Hard cheeses, rabbit, pasta.

■ **Aleatico** (al-ee-YA-tee-koh) **VARIETY**
This deeply coloured Italian grape is found mainly in Latium, Apulia and Corsica, as well as Eastern Europe. Usually seen as a varietal and occasionally as a fortified wine, it shows mainly *Muscat*-like aromas, and may be a *Muscat* mutation. Used mainly for fragrant, sweet wines but falling into disuse.

■ **Alicante (Bouschet)** (ah-lee-kahnt boo-shay) **VARIETY**
One of several important teinteurier grapes used to add colour to blends, for which it was developed. Found in Languedoc and Provence as well as Spain, where it's known as Garnacha Tintorera, it also grows in Eastern Europe, North Africa and, to some degree, California. Occasionally seen as an undistinguished varietal.
Descriptors High alcohol and deeply coloured, but can be flabby, showing little character on its own.

■ **Amarone** (AH-muh-ROH-neh) **BLEND**
A speciality of the Veneto region, Amarone is a style of *Valpolicella* made from selected and partially dried Recioto grapes. The most well known is Amarone delle Valpolicella *Recioto*.
Descriptors The wines are deep, dark, thick, intense and usually dry to off-dry, although the Amabile version is fairly sweet,
58 with rich dark fruit and raisin flavours and soft tannins.

Food Matches Game casseroles, parmesan, roast beef, rich stews.

■ Aramon VARIETY

A workhorse grape found in France's Languedoc-Rousillon region where its main strength is its disease resistance. Tends to produce rustic, pale, thin wines, and so is usually blended with more substantial grapes. Also found in Argentina, it is now losing ground to *Carignan*.

■ Auxerrois (oaks-air-wah/oh-sehr-wah) VARIETY

One of nearly 400 names given to *Malbec,* used mainly in Cahors. (ALSO SEE THE WHITE GRAPE AUXERROIS.)

■ Baco Noir (BAH-coh nwar) HYBRID

This French-American hybrid of Folle Blanche and the North American Riparia (Riverbank) grape is now grown mostly in eastern North America. Once common in Cognac, it has been banned from quality European vineyards. Can produce light and fruity wines, similar to *Beaujolais* (SEE GAMAY), or a more deeply pigmented, full-bodied-though-rustic *Bordeaux* style. Baco ages well – 5 to 10 years or more – and benefits from time in barrel, often American oak. Some consider Baco to be the red grape that best expresses the terroir of Ontario's Niagara region.

Descriptors Smoke, plums, blackberries, coffee, leather, and sometimes herbaceous aromas, with high acidity, deep colour and moderate tannins. Usually quite meaty.

Food Matches Hamburgers, kebabs, roast beef, game, curries, old cheddar, teriyaki, black beans, tomato sauces, pizza, lamb, firm cheeses.

■ Baga (BAH-guh) VARIETY

An important grape in many Portuguese wine regions including Bairrada, Dao, Douro and Ribetejo. Also called Tinta Bairrada, it produces dark, tannic, powerful and age-worthy wines.

Descriptors Dark, full-bodied, fruity and well structured, with high tannin and acid. Usually of average overall quality it seems to require a more modern approach to vinification.

Food Matches Pork, ragout, aubergine, burgers, moussaka, lamb.

■ Barbaresco APPELLATION

Along with *Barolo,* one of the great wines of Piedmont in Northwest Italy. Made near the town of Barbaresco entirely from the *Nebbiolo* grape, the wines are a shade lighter and earlier maturing than Barolo.

Descriptors SEE NEBBIOLO.

Food Matches Dim sum, roast game, beef, mushrooms.

■ Barbera (bar-BARE-uh) VARIETY

Barbera is the second most important red grape in Piedmont, Italy, after *Nebbiolo*. It usually appears as a varietal, with the better examples coming from Alba, Asti and Monferrato. The most famous is Barbera d'Asti. Although it has travelled to Argentina and parts of the US – mainly California – it is often relegated to a minor blending grape. Barbera wines range from light quaffers to big and age-worthy wines. In general it gets too little respect, although California and Piedmont both appear to be taking the grape more seriously.

Descriptors Distinctively Italian in character, with a sharp acidity, high alcohol and moderate to high tannin. Aromas suggest herbs, liquorice, sour cherry, and usually smokey oak.

Food Matches An ideal pizza and spaghetti wine that also works well with dark meats, anchovies, BBQ, charcuterie, chicken cacciatore, lamb stew, mozzarella, osso bucco, parmigiano, pesto, risotto.

■ Bardolino (BAR-doh-LEE-noh) APPELLATION

An important blended wine from Italy's Veneto region. Made primarily from *Corvina, Molinara* and *Rondinella* grapes, it is a simple-though-flavourful every day quaffer. Also made in a rosé style called Bardolino Chiaretto (KEE-ar-REH-toh), and sometimes seen as a "Novello" style. (ALSO SEE VALPOLICELLA.)

Descriptors Light bodied with a firm acidity and soft tannins, dominated by cherry aromas.

Food Matches Tuna, antipasti, cannelloni, pasta, tomato sauces.

■ **Barolo** (bar-OH-loh)   APPELLATION

Barolo is one of the most noble of the Italian red wines and
commands suitably high prices. The wine is named after the
town of Barolo, in Piedmont, and it is only on Barolo's hill-
sides that the autumn morning mists – the nebbia – cause
an almost magical change in the ripening *Nebbiolo* grapes.
Indeed, Nebbiolo doesn't seem to work as well anywhere but
in Piedmont. (Also SEE BARBARESCO.)

Descriptors SEE NEBBIOLO.

Food Matches Tournedos, beef fillet, venison stew, steak with
mushrooms, game stews.

■ **Bastardo** (bas-TAR-doh)   VARIETY

An important but somewhat undistinguished grape of Portugal, where it makes up a significant portion of Port, Dao
and Bairrada. A little is grown in Madeira. In the vineyard it
produces high sugar but not much else.

■ **Beaujolais** (boh-zhoh-lay)   APPELLATION

Gamay is the only red grape grown in this southern-most
sub-region of Burgundy, where it produces three main quality
categories: simple, everyday Beaujolais; Beaujolais Villages;
and substantial and age-worthy Cru Beaujolais. The third
Thursday of November is celebrated world-wide as Beaujolais
Nouveau day, when barely-ready, somewhat frivolous wines
are released with much fanfare. (New World regions follow
suit with "Gamay Nouveau".)

■ **Bikaver/Egri Bikaver**   STYLE

Literally "bull's blood from Eger", Bikaver is one of Hungary's
best known wines, made mainly from the *Kekfrankos* grape.
Although the name suggests a robust wine, it is good but rather middle-of-the-road.

■ **Blauburgunder/Blauer Burgunder**   VARIETY

Along with Spätburgunder, a German synonym for *Pinot
Noir.*

■ Blaufränkisch VARIETY

Known as *Limberger* in Germany and *Kekfrankos* in Hungary, this grape goes back as far as Charlemagne, and is the most important red grape in Austria. It is called "Frankisch" as a tribute to its Franken origin, and at one time was thought to be *Gamay*. Grown in the US since the 1940s, it has become somewhat important in Washington State. Makes some excellent varietal wines in Austria and is also used in blending.

Descriptors Fruity, often juicy, with aromas of raspberry, white pepper, beetroot and spice. Dry, with medium tannins, it can be almost *Zinfandel*-like, but more often is light and velvety, with a pronounced acidity. Can mature to an elegant smoothness.

Food Matches Beef Bourguignonne, beef stroganoff, moussaka, sausage.

■ Bordeaux (Rouge) APPELLATION

Considered the pinnacle, if not the best, in red wine, Bordeaux is a blend of *Cabernet Sauvignon, Cabernet Franc, Merlot* and, less often these days, *Malbec* and *Petite Verdot*. Actually the blend can vary from 80% *Cabernet Sauvignon* to 90-95% *Merlot*. Some of these classic wines are revered, coveted, very expensive, and can even be worth the price. However, the buyer is advised to shop carefully as many mediocre wines trade on Bordeaux's traditional prestige.

Descriptors It's hard to typify Bordeaux given the different representation of the three dominant grapes. In general, look for a biggish, rich wine laden with dark berry aromas and ample spice, often from new oak. The robe is dark, moving toward brick with age, and hefty tannins enable it to age for 10 to 20 years or more.

Food Matches BBQ red meats, lamb, beef, beef stroganoff, sausages, kangaroo, meatloaf, sirloin, game meats. (ALSO SEE Cabernet, Merlot, Meritage.)

■ Brown Muscat VARIETY

This dark-skinned *Muscat* grape is found almost exclusively in Australia where it is used to produce Liqueur Muscat, a splendidly rich, fortified dessert wine.

Descriptors Intensely sweet and viscous with a slight sherrified note.

Food Matches Christmas pudding, mince pie, chocolate mousse, cherry or orange based desserts.

■ Brunello di Montalcino   VARIETY
(brew-NELL-oh dee MON-tahl-CHEE-noh)

A clone of *Sangiovese* Grosso, the Brunello grape is unique to Tuscany and produces the wine of the same name. Rosso di Montalcino is a less ambitious version that is ready to drink sooner, and is correspondingly less expensive. *Brunello* has a brownish hue to the skin, hence the name, and produces massive, tannic wines that can take years to soften.

Descriptors Aromas suggest floral, tar, spices, and earth. Big, hard, tannic, jammy, yet flavourful, and tremendously age-worthy, 10-20 years on average.

Food Matches Requires equally rugged foods: roast beef, rabbit, lamb, game, aged and hard cheeses, tomato sauces, mushroom stew.

■ Cabernet Franc (ca-ber-nay frahN)   VARIETY

Now known to be one of the parents of *Cabernet Sauvignon,* "Cab Franc" is a significant component in *Bordeaux* and *Meritage* blends, adding perfume and softness. Serves as an insurance grape in France when Cab Sauv fails to ripen adequately. Important in Loire's Bourgueil region where, as Le Breton, it produces substantial and age-worthy wines. The grape travels well and can be found in Ontario, South America, Australia, California, Washington State, and New Zealand. It is an up-and-coming variety as more regions learn how to coax substance out of this friendly noble grape. Often used for rosé wines such as Rose d'Anjou.

Descriptors Aromatic, with soft tannins and a somewhat tangy acidity. Medium to full bodied and fruity, with a pronounced herbaceous quality. Aromas can include raspberries, strawberries, violets, cocoa, cedar, spice, leather, dill, and pencil box.

Food Matches Good food choices are cheddar, duck, goulash, jugged hare, lamb, pork chops, osso bucco, pulled pork, quail, roast beef, old flavourful cheeses, roast poultry, sausages, smoked eel, frikadellen, shepherd's pie.

■ Cabernet Sauvignon   **VARIETY**
(ca-ber-nay soh-vee-nyon)

Often considered the most noble of the French grapes, Cabernet is the main component of the long-lived *Bordeaux* blend, where some believe it achieves its greatest stature, if not greatest expression. Exceptional examples also come from California and Australia. Most wine regions grow at least some Cab, producing bold, full-bdied wines. Can be extraordinary and is usually priced accordingly, although budget versions can often be a waste of money. New World blends in the Bordeaux style are sometimes called *meritage,* although varietal names seem to dominate store shelves. (In some regions, a wine labelled "Cabernet" can be Cab Sauv, Cab Franc or a blend of both.)

Descriptors   Supple, aromatic and big-bodied, with complex aromas that can include ripe plum, blackberry, black pepper, mint, dark chocolate, clove, cinnamon, cassis, blackcurrant, cedar, green pepper, cigar box, and pencil shavings. With substantial colour, tannins and structure, it is one of the most age-worthy wines, anywhere from 5-50 years.

Food Matches   Roast beef, beef wellington, brie, camembert, chili, game, garlic, gorgonzola, haggis, lasagne, mature hard cheeses, meat loaf, meaty casseroles, osso bucco, partridge, quail, roast lamb, sausage, spaghetti, steak, beef tenderloin.

■ Cahors   **APPELLATION**
SEE MALBEC.

■ Canaiolo (Nero) (can-ay-YOH-loh)   **VARIETY**
Grown throughout Italy, this little-known grape is one of the accepted red grapes for *Chianti* in Tuscany, adding softness to counter-balance the bolder *Sangiovese*. Mainly a blending grape, somewhat bland and bitter, it can be nurtured into a decent varietal.

■ Cannonau   **VARIETY**
This is the name given to a variety of *Grenache* in Sardinia, where the grape produces the excellent, full-bodied and deeply tannic varietal, Cannonau de Sardegna, as well as sweet, rosé and fortified wines.

■ Carignan(e)/Cariñena   VARIETY
(car-IN-yan/CAR-in-NYAY-nuh)

The ubiquitous grape of Frances's Languedoc-Rousillon region, Carignan is important throughout France, and is abundant in Minervois and Corbiéres. It is also found in North Africa, the Priorato region of Spain, and in California where it is used to create mainly jug wines (E.g. "California burgundy"). Although mostly used for blending, usually with *Grenache,* it can make a decent varietal, especially from low-yielding "old" vines. It can suffer from coarseness when young, and yet it rarely ages well.

Descriptors   Richly tannic and acidic, with concentrated fruit, good colour, body and depth, but little flavour and aroma.

Food Matches   Ratatouille, lamb, liver, sausage, tomato sauces, steak, cassoulet.

■ Carménère/Grand Vidure (car-men-air)   VARIETY
This venerable Bordeaux grape fell out of favour when less troublesome varieties became more common. It has travelled some, but has found its best home in Chile where it produces deep, full-bodied wines with lots of fruit and spice. For many years *Carménère* was mistaken for *Merlot* in Chile, and it is now emerging as one of that country's star grapes.

Descriptors   Deeply coloured, full bodied, rich and jammy, with moderate tannins and aromas of blackcurrants.

Food Matches   SEE MERLOT.

■ Cencibel (sen-seh-bell)   VARIETY
An alternate name for *Tempranillo* in central and southern Spain (La Mancha, Valdapeñas).

■ Chambourcin (sham-boor-saN)   HYBRID
Originally from the Loire Valley, this French Hybrid grape is not approved for use in France. Some limited plantings exist in Australia and Canada. A heavy bearer, Chambourcin has good colour, flavour and body, somewhat reminiscent of *Beaujolais.* Also used to produce rosé wines, it has a strong following in cold climate regions where vine survival is an issue. As a blending grape or on its own, it has excellent potential for the future.

■ Chancellor   HYBRID

A French hybrid that flourished briefly before 1940 but is now almost unknown. Some experimental plantings exist in Canada's BC region, where it is used as a blending grape. Has a following among cool climate amateur winemakers. Rather bland though fruity.

■ Charbono/Charbonneau (shar-bone-noh)   VARIETY

Peculiar to California, mainly in Napa, this grape may be related to Piedmont's *Dolcetto,* and produces concentrated red wines that are tannic and acidic yet somewhat dull.

■ Châteauneuf-du-Pape   APPELLATION/BLEND
(sha-toe-nuff-doo-pap)

Named for the "new chateau" of Pope Clement V in the 14th century, this high-end blend of up to 13 different grapes is one of the most recognized wines of the Rhône. *Grenache* and *Syrah* dominate the blend, creating a dependable, elegant and age-worthy wine, though often unexceptional, and it can be overly expensive. (A little Châteauneuf-du-Pape Blanc is made from Clairette, Bourboulenc and Grenache Blanc.)

Descriptors   SEE GRENACHE, SYRAH.

Food Matches   Coq au Vin, beef casserole, duck, goose, seasonal turkey, steak tartar, cabbage rolls, game.

■ Chianti (kee-YON-tee)   APPELLATION/BLEND

Dating from the 12th century, Chianti is one of the oldest established wine traditions. A blend of up to five indigenous grapes, dominated by *Sangiovese,* it ranges from ho-hum, rustic "peasant" wines presented in straw covered "fiasci" to rich, powerful Classico and Riserva, suitable for ageing well past a decade. Recently *Cabernet* has made an appearance in the blend, with the result usually called a "Super Tuscan".

Descriptors   Ruby red with aromas of roses, cherries, violets, earth, and tar. Usually medium to full bodied with mild tannins, although Classico and Riserva can be quite formidable.

Food Matches   Red meat casseroles, parmesan, mozzarella, tomato sauces, game, goose.

■ **Cinsaut/Cinsault** (san-soh)   **VARIETY**

This centuries-old grape is similar to *Grenache* in character and is important in the Languedoc in the South of France as well as South Africa. A versatile blending partner, it adds colour and softness. Often found in Tavel rosé and *Châteauneuf-du-Pape,* it is just as apt to become a bulk wine. One of the parents of South Africa's *Pinotage,* where it was once commonly known as "Hermitage", it is also found in Corbiéres and Minervois blends. Not often seen as a varietal.

Descriptors   Light, fresh, soft and aromatic with light colour and low tannins, a floral nose and very good body. Matures in bottle up to 5 years.

Food Matches   Ratatouille, lamb, stuffed tomatoes, sausage.

■ **Concord**   **VARIETY**

The original North American *Labrusca* or "fox" grape, Concord sets the standard for juice, jams, jellies and grape flavoured gum, but is not very convincing as a wine as it never loses that Welch's aroma and flavour. Grows abundantly in Canada and the US, and although still popular as a sacramental wine, it is thankfully falling into disuse. Not acceptable under Ontario's VQA wine laws. Also a good eating grape.

Descriptors   Quite grapey with very little tannin, but capable of good body and acidity. Usually off-dry to medium sweet.

■ **Corvina**   **VARIETY**

An important grape in Veneto, Italy, where it is a main ingredient in all forms of *Valpolicella* and *Bardolino,* by blending with *Rondinella, Molinara* and *Malvoisie.* When dried to partial raisins, it goes into the luscious *Amarone* and *Recioto.* Rarely seen as a varietal.

Descriptors/Food Matches   SEE VALPOLICELLA.

■ **Cot**   **VARIETY**

SEE MALBEC.

■ **De Chaunac/Dechaunac** (dee shoh-nak)   **HYBRID**

Originally known as Siebel 9459, this Hybrid grape was named in honour of Adhemar de Chaunac, winemaster and director of research from 1944-1961 at Brights Winery in Ontario.

Descriptors/Food Matches   SEE MARECHAL FOCH.

■ **Dolcetto** (dohl-CHEH-toh)   VARIETY

Although the name Dolcetto means "little sweet one", the wines are mainly dry, often substantial, and perhaps the ideal every day wine. Almost exclusive to Italy, the grape grows in some of the least promising areas of Piedmont. Sometimes compared to *Beaujolais,* but somewhat richer, it is usually bottled as a varietal, with Dolcetto d'Alba being one of the best known. Enjoy it in its youth as it does not age well.

Descriptors   Highly coloured with a purplish hue. Very fruity and fragrant with aromas of bitter cherry, chocolate and licorice. Lightly tannic, good body and concentrated, with a bit of a bite.

Food Matches   Antipasti, cold cuts, stuffed peppers, mozzarella, white truffle, pizza, pasta with red sauce, poultry, light meats, risotto, fontina.

■ **Dornfelder**   VARIETY

A European cross between Helfensteiner and Heroldrebe, dating from 1956 and found mainly in Germany, Dornfelder usually appears as a varietal and seems to be gaining in popularity.

Descriptors   Deeply coloured with aromatic berry fruit, good acidity, medium to full body and ample tannin. Good when young and able to handle oak ageing.

Food Matches   Hearty roasts, game, flavourful cheeses. (Also SEE *GAMAY*.)

■ **Durif** (dur-reef)   VARIETY

An undistinguished grape that has almost disappeared from its French homeland. Once thought to be the same grape as *Petite Sirah*.

■ **Freisa** (FRAY-zuh)   VARIETY

A versatile grape grown in Piedmont where it produces all manner of pale wines, from dry to sweet to frizzante. Regaining some of its past popularity.

■ **Gamay (Noir Jus Blanc)**   VARIETY

This, the *Beaujolais* grape, is the only red grape grown in that region of Burgundy, where it produces Beaujolais ranging from "Nouveau" to substantial Cru versions. The grape has

68 found but a few homes outside of France, notably in Ontario's

Niagara where it can often outperform its European counterparts. It can also be found in Eastern Europe, Italy and South Africa, and a little is grown in the Loire valley. Gamay also comes in a Teinturier variety that is quite rare. (Also SEE PASSE-TOUT-GRAINS.)

Descriptors Fruity aromas of cherry, raspberry and strawberry, with a hint of pepper. Typically light bodied with soft tannins and often a light oakiness. Better examples can be substantial and age-worthy up to five years.

Food Matches Pork chops, charcuterie, veal, hamburgers, liver, salami, kebabs, ham, baked poultry, chicken salad, grilled veg, tex-mex, grilled or poached salmon or trout, soft cheeses, pizza, pasta.

■ Gamay Beaujolais   VARIETY

This name is found only in California to refer to a grape that has no relation to *Gamay,* and that appears to be an obscure *Pinot Noir* clone.

■ Garnacha (Tinta)   VARIETY

The Spanish and possibly original name for *Grenache*.

■ Gattinara   APPELLATION

A name given to *Nebbiolo* in the Gattinara sub-region of North-western Piedmont.

■ Graciano/Graciana   VARIETY

(gra-see-anno/grat-see-anna)

Mainly used to add flavour to Spanish Rioja, this low-yielding grape can also be found in Navarra, with a few tiny plantings in Southern France. In California it is called Xeres. While its use is waning in traditional areas, Languedoc and Mendoza are now having some success with it.

Descriptors Deeply coloured with aromas of spice, plum and perfume. Good extract and tannin with high acidity. Quite age-worthy.

Food Matches SEE *TEMPRANILLO*.

■ Grenache (Noir)/Garnacha/Cannonau   VARIETY
(greh-nosh; gar-NA-chuh)

Thought to have originated in Spain as Garnacha Tinta, this under-recognized grape migrated to Southern France to become one of the most widely planted red grapes there. It is the number two red grape in Spain where it is blended with *Tempranillo* to create the red wines of Rioja, Penedés, Priorato and Navarra. Also expect to find Grenache dominating Côte-du-Rhône wines, Tavel, Banyuls and *Châteauneuf-du-Pape* (up to 65%). Widely used to produce rosé and rosado wines, the grape revels in hot climates and has found suitable soil in Australia (where it is often blended with *Shiraz* and *Mourvedre*) and California. Not common as a varietal, but this is changing.

Descriptors   Pale, a bit rustic, with aromas of pepper, toast, ripe plums, lavender, and thyme. Somewhat soft with firm tannins. Juicy, fruity, dense and meaty on the palate, and may have an impression of sweetness. It can be simple when young but can age well.

Food Matches   Beef stew or casserole, sausage, chili, steak tartar, stuffed tomatoes, roast vegetables, lamb, BBQ.

■ Grignolino (GRIN-yoh-LEE-noh)   VARIETY
Found mainly in Piedmont and North-western Italy as well as California, the vine produces a varietal wine that is easy drinking and best when young. It is difficult to grow, which tends to discourage its cultivation, so it is fairly uncommon. Often compared to *Dolcetto*.

Descriptors   A dry, light-bodied, everyday wine with mainly strawberry aromas, often with high acid and tannins.

■ Kadarka   VARIETY
The second most important red grape in Hungary, especially the Szekszard region, where it is an ingredient in "Bull's Blood" (SEE EGRI BIKAVER). Not as important as it once was, and is losing ground to *Kekfrankos* (Blaufrankisch). Also found in Austria and Yugoslavia, as well as Bulgaria where it is called Gamza. Somewhat temperamental in the vineyard.

Descriptors   If yields are kept down and the grape is allowed to ripen, it can produce full-bodied, deeply coloured and tannic wines that show spicy aromas.

70 **Food Matches**   Sausages, goulash, souvlaki, moussaka.

■ Kékfrankos
VARIETY

The name given to *Blaufränkisch* in Hungary, where the grape produces deep, substantial red wines.

Descriptors Aromas suggest dark berries and pepper; juicy and full bodied with good colour. Good when young or with mid-term ageing.

Food Matches Beef bourgogne, beef stroganoff, moussaka, sausage, tomato sauces.

■ Labrusca (luh-BROO-skuh)
VARIETY

The ubiquitous grape species that is native to Eastern North America. Best known variety is the *Concord,* which makes great jams, jellies and juices, but is plagued by the so-called Foxy aroma. Has a somewhat dedicated following but is now banned under most appellation systems. Sometimes used for fortified and sacramental wines. The main white variety is the *Niagara*.

■ Lambrusco (lam-BROO-skoh)
VARIETY

Found mainly in the Emiglia-Romagna region and the lower Po Valley in Northern Italy, Lambrusco makes the light red sparkling wine of the same name. Lambrusco de Sorbara is the highest quality, with Lambrusco Salamino a close second. A sub-variety, Castelvetro, produces a similar though less substantial wine. Not to be confused with *Labrusca*.

Descriptors Fruity, slightly tart, often a bit sweet, with moderate tannins. Altogether cheerful and intended for immediate consumption.

Food Matches Can work well with red meats, white meats, parma ham, salami, and flavourful cheeses. Better to avoid with fish. Also a very good aperitif and perfect with meatloaf or strawberry fool.

■ Lemberger/Limberger
VARIETY

Known as *Blaufrankisch* in Austria, Lemberger is also somewhat important in Germany where it contributes to light coloured, early drinking blended wines. Can also be found in Hungary, as *Kekfrankos,* and Yugoslavia.

■ **Leon Millot** (lay-oN mee-yoh)   HYBRID

Developed by Eugene Kuhlmann, Leon Millot is a "sister" grape to *Maréchal Foch* and Lucy Kuhlmann. All three produce similar wines, with this and Lucy Kuhlman being somewhat lighter and less acidic than Foch. Can be very good if treated with care.

■ **Lucy Kuhlmann**   HYBRID

SEE MARÉCHAL FOCH.

■ **Malbec** (mahl-bek)   VARIETY

Once known as Cot in Bordeaux, and sometimes called *Auxerrois,* Malbec was once considered indispensable to the red *Bordeaux* formula. Now found mostly in blends in the Loire region, and in Cahors, where it is called "black wine", it constitutes the bulk of the red wine bearing that region's name. There are a few plantings in Spain's Ribera del Duero, California and Chile, but Malbec's spiritual home must be Argentina, where it produces luscious, character-filled and age-worthy wines. French versions show elegance, while the best Argentinean samples are rich and jammy. May be added to *Meritage.*

Descriptors   Often described as a rustic Merlot, Malbec produces dark, juicy, flavourful wines with high extract, low acid and low to moderate tannins. Aromas include blackberry, plums, spice and a slightly gamey note. Can age well.

Food Matches   Steak and kidney pie, lamb shanks, beef en croute, beef wellington, game, mature hard cheeses, cabbage rolls, duck a l'orange, truffles, steak tartar.

■ **Malvasia (Nero/Nera)** (mahl-vuh-SEE-uh)   VARIETY

This grape was known to the ancient Greeks but today is rather scarce (the white version is more plentiful). Found mainly in Italy, especially Aldo Adige and Piedmont, and there are small plantings in Portugal and Northern Spain. Gradually falling into disuse.

Descriptors   Usually used for blending, Malvasia Nero on its own can produce a dark, aromatic, high alcohol varietal wine with good character.

■ **Maréchal Foch** (mar-shel foash)　　　　**HYBRID**

This French hybrid, developed by Eugene Kuhlmann, was named in honour of Field Marshal Foch (which does not explain the proliferation of spellings: Marechal, Mareshal, Marshal, Marichel, Marichal). Once widespread in the Loire, where it helped to revive the French wine industry after phylloxera, Foch is now vina non gratta there. It has a strong following in New York State and in Canada, where some vintners make premium "Old Vines Foch". Winter hardy and early ripening, it does well in cooler climates. Often found as a varietal, it is also used for blending and jug wines. Created in the Oberlin Institute in Alsace around 1915 by crossing "Riparia x Rupestris" with Goldriesling.

Descriptors　Dark, purpley hued, with distinctive herbaceous, pepper, plum and blueberry aromas. Medium to full bodied with light tannins and a forward acidity. Good but not usually premium quality and can be oaked. Best when young as it often doesn't age well, 4-5 years at most.

Food Matches　Asiago, gouda, tomato sauces, pizza, rare beef, veal, burgers, game birds.

■ **Mataro/Monestrell**　　　　**VARIETY**

See Mourvedre.

■ **Mavrodaphne**　　　　**VARIETY**

Found only in Greece, mainly Corinth, the "black laurel" grape produces a fullish bodied wine that is usually oaked. Occasionally it is made into a sweet fortified wine of the same name.

■ **Mavrud**　　　　**VARIETY**

Peculiar to the Balkans and Bulgaria, Mavrud produces an intense, robust and tannic wine that can benefit from oak, although it does not age well.

Food Matches　Beef stroganoff, goulash, roast lamb.

■ **Meritage**　　　　**BLEND**

This American term was coined by combining merit and heritage to denote premium wines made in the *Bordeaux* tradition, using the standard Bordeaux grapes: *Cabernet Sauvignon, Merlot, Cabernet Franc, Malbec* and *Petite Verdot* for red wines; *Sauvignon Blanc, Semillon* and *Muscadelle* for white wines. (Rhymes with heritage.)　　　73

■ **Merlot** (mair-loh)   VARIETY

Merlot is the most planted red grape in *Bordeaux*. It is an essential part of the region's blends and, in fact, can account for 90% and even 100% of some Bordeaux wines. Like the other noble grapes of Bordeaux, Merlot travels well and shows its character wherever it's planted. It's appreciated for its smoothness on the palate, soft tannins, long life, affinity for oak, and "fruit bomb" profile, all of which make it an ideal partner for blending with *Cabernet*. Merlot is very popular as a standalone varietal.

Descriptors   Rich, elegant, and fruity. Aromas include dark plums, herbs, spices, liquorice, blackberries, and blackcurrants. Valued for its softness and drinkability, showing soft tannins, a smooth palate and an ageing ability approaching that of Cabernet.

Food Matches   Asiago, baba ganough, bean stew, blue cheese, liver, duck, gouda, grilled meats, tuna, lamb stew, mushroom sauces, pasta with meat sauce, pork chops, rack of lamb, chévre, roast beef, soft ripe cheeses.

■ **Mission**   VARIETY

One of the original Californian grapes, Mission was apparently named for the Jesuit monks who planted it there in the 1700s for use as a sacramental wine. Although the grape's precise history is unknown, there is some opinion that it originated in Spain, and it appears to be the same grape as the Pais of Chile. Falling into disuse because of its susceptibility to phylloxera and the ordinariness of the wine.

■ **Mondeuse (Noire)**   VARIETY

While some think that the grape is the same as the Refosco of Friuli and Venezia, Mondeuse is undoubtedly the most important grape in the Savoie-Bugey region of Eastern France. Also grown in Argentina, Australia, California, and Oregon, this somewhat under-rated grape is capable of producing substantial and distinctive wines. Occasionally it is blended with *Gamay* or *Pinot Noir* in an effort to contain its voluptuous nature. The wines can age particularly well, especially in oak barrels.

Descriptors   Very high quality and deeply coloured, the wines show concentrated plum flavours, with loads of tannin, prominent acidity, and a slightly bitter finish.

Food Matches   Lamb, roasted garlic, roasted duck, potatoes au gratin.

■ **Monestrell**   VARIETY

A Spanish synonym for Mourvedre.

■ **Montepulciano (d'Abruzzi)**   VARIETY

(MON-tay-pool-CHAH-noh da BROOT-tsee)

Originally from Tuscany, the Montepulciano grape is now found throughout Central Italy, especially Abruzzi and the Marches. Mainly appears as a varietal, although it is sometimes used for blending. (Also SEE SANGIOVESE.)

Descriptors   Deeply coloured, usually with high acid and alcohol. Somewhat rustic, showing aromas of blackberry, pepper and spices with moderate tannins. Can be very age worthy.

Food Matches   Béchamel sauce, lasagne, olives, pasta, pizza, salami, stuffed peppers, veal chops, kidney.

■ **Mourvèdre** (moor-ved)   VARIETY

Possibly originating in Spain, Mourvedre is an important blending grape in France, especially with *Syrah* and *Grenache*. Important in Southern Rhône wines, including *Châteauneuf-du-Pape,* Mourvèdre is also planted in Languedoc, Bandol, Provence, California, and Australia. Called Monastrell or Mataro in Spain, it is now making a major statement in Chile.

Descriptors   Deeply coloured, with aromas of herbs, spices, blackberries, and black currants. Intensely fruity and fleshy, somewhat gamey, with high alcohol and low acidity. Hard and earthy when young, maturing to smoke and leather. Can age up to 20 years.

Food Matches   Ribs, herbs de provence, lamb chops, BBQ, cream or pepper sauces, tarragon chicken, venison, roast veg, game, smoked ham.

■ **Müllerrebe** (MOOL-er-RAY-beh)   VARIETY

The German name for *Pinot Meunier*.

■ **Nebbiolo** (neh-BYOH-loh)   VARIETY

The only grape found in the legendary *Barolo* and *Barbaresco* wines of northern Piedmont, as well as Nebbiolo d'Alba, this demanding and assertive fruit produces dense and complex wines that typically must spend at least 5 years in bottle to develop their characteristic velvety richness (10 to 20 years is not unusual). The grape is beginning to appear in other wine regions, but generally falls short of Italy's examples. Also known as Spanna, Gattinara, Ghemme.

Descriptors   Exotic aromas of violets, prunes, bitter chocolate, roses, truffles, tobacco, licorice, camphor, and "goudron" (tar). Very full bodied with firm, muscular tannins. Somewhat colour challenged.

Food Matches   Rare roast beef, game, truffles, wild or porcini mushrooms, beef bourguignon, grouse/pheasant, osso bucco, rich stews, parmesan, aubergine, top steak, parma ham.

■ **Negroamaro**   VARIETY

This is the sixth most important red grape in Southern Italy, especially in the province of Apulia and the DOC region of Salice Salentino. Although often relegated to blending, the grape can produce substantial, ageworthy, high-alcohol varietal wines as well as agreeable rosés.

Descriptors   Dark, intense, often jammy, with dark berry, cherry and prune flavours and moderate tannins.

Food Matches   Tex-Mex, sausages, tomato sauces.

■ **Nero d'Avola** (NEE-roh DA-voh-luh)   VARIETY

This little known grape is the number one red wine producer in Sicily, where it has been grown for several hundred years. The wines are high in quality and age-worthy, although Novello wines are produced each year for release in November. Thought to be the best expression of Sicilian terroir.

Descriptors   Usually dark and rich, possibly jammy, with aromas of red fruits, blackberries and pepper, and substantial tannins. Sometimes blended into Marsala.

Food Matches   Ragu, red meats, duck, roasted red peppers, mozzarella, grilled steak, caramelised onions, hard cheeses.

■ Norton/Cynthiana   VARIETY

One of the oldest "native" North American winegrapes, Norton may in fact be a hybrid that developed in the wild when an imported vinifera species came in contact with native vitis Aestivalis grapes. Whatever its parentage, Norton is an important grape in the middle states of the US, where it creates an excellent *Merlot*-like wine. Often called "*Cabernet* of the Ozarks".

Descriptors   Rich and earthy, with aromas of raspberry and spice, and very good body.

Food Matches   SEE MERLOT.

■ Pais (pay)   VARIETY
SEE MISSION.

■ Passe-tout-grains/Passetoutgrains   STYLE
(pass-too-gran)

This lesser blend from the Mâconnais region of Burgundy consists of not less than 30% *Pinot Noir* and the balance made up of *Gamay*. Not considered to be a noteworthy wine, although it can be a bargain and will improve in bottle for 2-4 years. Better examples can be quite good.

■ Periquita (PAIR-ih-KEE-tuh)   VARIETY

An important grape in Portugal where it is responsible for flavourful, light to medium bodied reds of the same name. Can benefit from a bit of bottle time. May be a blend or a varietal.

■ Petite Sirah (peh-teet ser-rah)   VARIETY

Not to be confused with Syrah or Shiraz – to which it is no relation – Petit Sirah is possibly several grapes of undetermined origin. For some time it was thought to be Durif or even a *Pinot Noir* clone. Very popular in California and Mexico, where it produces distinctive varietals that can resemble Rhône wines (which may account for the name). Can also be found in Argentina. Sometimes added to *Zinfandel*.

Descriptors   Deeply coloured with aromas of pepper, perfume, violets and earth. Full bodied and juicy, with rich tannins. Can produce an exceptional, sometimes huge, wine that ages well.

Food Matches   Treat as *Syrah* or *Zinfandel*.

■ **Petit Verdot** (peh-tee verr-doh)   **VARIETY**

This classic *Bordeaux* variety is acceptable in the traditional blend, though it is not as popular as it once was. There are some limited plantings in Napa as well as Ontario, where it is made into a varietal wine when not incorporated into *Meritage* blends. Seems to be making a bit of a comeback.

Descriptors Deeply coloured with aromas of pepper and spice. Concentrated, verging on powerful, with firm tannins. Can be tart in off years. Quite age-worthy.

Food Matches SEE ZINFANDEL.

■ **Pignolo** (pin-YOH-loh)   **VARIETY**

A native of Friuli, Italy, the grape covers limited ground and can produce full-bodied, deeply coloured, flavourful wines that respond well to oak ageing.

■ **Pinotage** (PEE-noh-TAHZH)   **VARIETY**

An important grape in South Africa and nowhere else, Pinotage is a cross of *Cinsaut* and *Pinot Noir*. Makes a light to medium bodied and distinctively aromatic wine. Much like *Beaujolais* when young, it can be more serious when aged in oak. For some it's an acquired taste.

Descriptors Inky coloured with aromas of berries, plums, earth and chocolate. Can have a peculiar paint-like aroma and a palate that is sometimes described as "dusty". Good longevity, although it matures early.

Food Matches Caramelised onions, felafel, beef wellington, chili, moussaka, roast beef, ham, pepper steak, guinea fowl.

■ **Pinot Meunier** (pee-noh muhn-yay)   **VARIETY**

A cousin of *Pinot Noir,* the "miller's" grape's main claim to fame is its importance in the production of Champagne. One of only three grapes allowed in that region, Pinot Meunier is valued for its reliability in the vineyard (vs. Pinot Noir) and it makes up about 40% of Champagne's grape plantings. Now found to some degree wherever champagne is emulated. Sometimes used to produce light red and rosé wines. Known as Müllerrebe in Germany.

Descriptors The grape can produce a youthful, fruity and light coloured table wine with aromas of plums, violets, spice and toasty oak, with high acidity and good body.

Food Matches Grilled sausage, burgers, steak, pizza, pasta with tomato sauce.

■ Pinot Noir (pee-noh nwar)   VARIETY

The grape responsible for the great red wines of Burgundy, Pinot Noir produces some of the world's most seductive wines, and in good years it produces some of the greatest and most expensive. Now finding good homes in many regions of the New World, especially New Zealand, Oregon and Canada. Usually oak aged, it is also used to produce red and rosé wines in Sancerre and "Blanc des Noirs" Champagne. Very food friendly.

Descriptors Aromas can be any of plum, cherry, spice, tobacco, leather, vegetal, raspberry, "barnyard", truffles, game, decaying leaves, and beetroot. Silky textured with lightish body and soft tannins. Can be age-worthy, up to 15 years or more in the best vintages, but 4-5 years is more typical.

Food Matches Roast poultry, charcuterie, beef bourguignon/wellington, shepherd's pie, roast pork, coq au vin, lamb, prime rib, filet mignon, meatier fish, tuna, grilled salmon, firm cheeses, parmesan, gorgonzola, tomatoes, mushroom risotto, pasta, escargot, chocolate.

■ Plavac Mali   VARIETY

Thought to be the same grape as California's *Zinfandel*, Plavac Mali is found throughout Croatia and the Dalmatian coast where it produces dense, dark, rustic, often heady wines that can be high in tannin.

■ Primitivo (PREE-mi-TEE-voh)   VARIETY

Prominent in Southern Italy, the Primitivo grape appears to be the original *Zinfandel*. Much like Zinfandel in character, but tends to be a bit lighter and more rustic. Often blended with local grapes, such as *Sangiovese,* and can even appear as a port style wine.

Descriptors/Food Matches SEE ZINFANDEL.

■ Refosco/Mondeuse   VARIETY

Refosco appears to be an ancient grape and is limited mainly to the Friuli and Colli Oriental districts of Italy. Makes an age-worthy wine that benefits from barrel treatment. Deeply coloured, with aromas of plums and almonds, good body, and high acidity.

■ Rondinella   VARIETY

Important in Italy's Veneto region where it plays a role in the *Valpolicella* blend. Somewhat low in flavour, and valued more for the quantity of grapes it produces. (SEE CORVINA.)

■ Rosso di Montalcino   APPELLATION
(ROH-soh dee MAHN-tahl-CHEE-noh)

This prized wine from the Montalcino subregion of Tuscany is made from the *Sangiovese* Grosso grape and is lesser brother to *Brunello*. The wine may be a second label for a Brunello producer or even a declassified Brunello. Lighter, fruitier, less austere and earlier maturing than Brunello, it can be quite tannic and acidic. Usually aged 6-18 months in oak (vs. 4 years for Brunello), it is far less costly than Brunello and usually good value.

Descriptors Cherries, blueberries, licorice and floral, often with a bit of tar, and formidable tannins.

Food Matches Roast poultry, game birds, Cornish hen, cutlets, chops.

■ Rotberger/Rottenberg   VARIETY

A cross of *Trollinger* and *Riesling,* this hardy, early ripening grape is suitable for marginal growing regions such as England. Rather scarce, it more resembles its Trollinger parent.

■ Ruby Cabernet   VARIETY

Developed in California by crossing *Carignan* and *Cabernet Sauvignon,* this underrated grape can produce a decent to excellent wine in a challenging warm climate. Can also be found in Argentina, Chile, Australia, and South Africa. Sometimes used as a tinting grape because of its deep colour.

Descriptors Deeply coloured, fruity and sometimes quite tannic, with good body.

Food Matches SEE DOLCETTO, BARBERA.

■ Ruby Red/Rubired   HYBRID

Popular in California, this red-fleshed hybrid grape sometimes appears as a varietal. It is useful as a blending grape where more colour is desired. Otherwise it serves a limited role.

■ **Sancerre** (sann-sair)   APPELLATION

The red wines of Sancerre are made from *Pinot Noir*, and tend to be a bit austere.

■ **Sangiovese** (san-joe-VAY-say)   VARIETY

The "Blood of Jove" grape reigns in the Tuscany region of Italy, where it is the basis of *Chianti* and several other wines including Vino Nobile di Montepulciano and *Brunello* di Montalcino. Main cultivars are Sangiovese Grosso, Sangiovese Piccolo, and Brunello. Grown in virtually all wine regions of Italy, it is also found in California where it makes a premium varietal wine, and is beginning to appear in Ontario.

Descriptors   Aromas can include cherries, truffles, earth, and irises. Medium to full bodied with high acidity and a solid tannic spine, it can be tremendously age worthy, 10-50 years.

Food Matches   Cold meats, light meat dishes, BBQ. Californian examples go well with roast pork, grilled steak, chicken cacciatore, parmesan, spinach & ricotta cannelloni, pizza, mushrooms, tomatoes, truffles, pork chops, stuffed eggplant.

■ **Spätburgunder** (SHPATE-ber-gun-der)   VARIETY

A German synonym for *Pinot Noir*.

■ **St. Laurent** (san lor-on)   VARIETY

Important in Eastern Europe, principally Austria, the vine may be related to *Pinot Noir,* but is better behaved in the vineyard. Often used as a blending grape, on its own St. Laurent can produced a rich, characterful and age-worthy wine. Also known as Vavrineke in Slovakia and Svatvovarinhi in the Czech Republic.

Descriptors   Dark, concentrated and flavourful with low tannins and a velvety palate. Aromas include cherries, earth and mushrooms, usually with a layer of oak. Can be slightly bitter.

Food Matches   SEE ZWEIGELT/PINOT NOIR.

■ Syrah/Shiraz   VARIETY

Known as Shiraz in Australia, where it produces rich, full-bodied wines, the Syrah grape is the mainstay of the Rhône region of Southern France, and is a major ingredient in Hermitage, *Châteauneuf-du-Pape* and Côte Rhôtie. As Shiraz it is the basis of Penfolds "Grange", a wine that put the grape on the map for Australia, where it previously garnered little respect. Stylistically, wines labelled Syrah tend to be more subtle, elegant and less obviously fruity than the jammy, fruit-forward wines called Shiraz. Grown in almost every wine region these days with great success, it can often be found in New World Rhône- and Bordeaux-style blends.

Descriptors Aromas include spice, blackberries, raspberries, white or black pepper, mulberry, smoke, and mineral. Muscular, concentrated and complex with soft tannins. Ageable 4-6 years, the best examples can go 10-15 years.

Food Matches Game, BBQ sauce, beef in red wine, liver, tandoori chicken, chicken cacciatore, wings, moussaka, venison, rich stews, roast goose or duck, turkey, chili con carne, lamb with rosemary, hard cheeses, blue cheeses, wild mushroom dishes, garlicky dishes, kangaroo, beef teriyaki.

■ Tannat   VARIETY

The Tannat grape has not ventured very far from its home in Eastern Europe, the main exceptions being Argentina and Uruguay. There are some isolated plantings in France, principally in Madiran, but interest there is on the decline. Tannat's main use is as a blending grape, often in place of *Merlot* in *Cabernet* blends. It appears frequently as a varietal wine that can be quite substantial and interesting.

Descriptors Can resemble *Nebbiolo* when young, with tough, astringent tannins, deep colour and big, spicy flavours. Look for aromas of raspberries, spices and usually oak.

Food Matches Duck, hearty stews.

■ Tempranillo/Cencibel   VARIETY

(tem-pruh-NEE-yoh/sen-suh-bell)

The workhorse and most important noble grape of Spain, Tempranillo is the main ingredient in the red wines of Rioja, Penedés and Ribera del Duero. The grape covers roughly 1/4 of Spain's vineyards, and thrives in that nation's challenging climate. Outside Spain it can be found in Portugal, where it is called *Tinta Roriz* and goes into Dao, Douro and Port. There are plantings in Languedoc, California (called Valdepeñas there), Argentina, Mexico, and South Africa, but Spain is where Tempranillo rules. Usually blended with *Garnacha* and *Carignan,* it can also be found partnered with *Cabernet Sauvignon* or standing alone as a varietal. The wine is usually aged in oak, and in Old World Spain may rest too long in American oak barrels.

Descriptors Often compared to Cabernet Sauvignon, with deep colour, high alcohol and bold flavours. Aromas include spice, blackberry, plum, strawberry, smoke, sandalwood, tobacco, blackcurrant, and vanilla. Highly concentrated with lightish tannins. Rich and age-worthy, or it can also be young and fresh.

Food Matches BBQ poultry, empañadas, game, goulash, hamburgers, mature or salty cheeses, olives, paella, pork loin, portobellos, roast lamb, Spanish flan, tapas, steak & kidney pie, moussaka.

■ Tinta Roriz   VARIETY

A Portuguese name for *Tempranillo,* especially in the Douro valley where it goes into Douro table wines and Port. Also found in Dao wines.

■ Touriga Franca/Francesa   VARIETY

One of the five recommended Port grapes, this native fruit is now being used alone as a very good varietal, or may be blended with *Touriga Naçional* and *Tinta Roriz* to create a *meritage* style. Found throughout Portugal's Douro Valley and Tras-os-Motes region.

Descriptors Darkly coloured and robust, with hearty tannins and a nose dominated by mulberries and roses.

■ Touriga Naçional   VARIETY

This is the important and well respected Portuguese grape that gives us some of their best wines: Dao, Port and Douro. Also used for red *Vinho Verde* and occasionally for varietals. A little can be found in Australia.

Descriptors Deeply coloured and perfumy, with fruity berry flavours. Concentrated with firm tannins and good body.

Food Matches Souvlaki, burgers, lamb, moussaka, and anything Portuguese.

■ **Trollinger** VARIETY

Sometimes called Black Hamburg, this ancient, rather ordinary German variety is grown mainly in the region of Wurthemburg, Germany. Known as Schiava in Italy, it is often seen as a table grape.

Descriptors Low in tannin with a fresh acidity and deep colour. A light, easy-drinking "vin du porch", it is rarely serious.

Food Matches Cheese, cold cuts.

■ **Trouseau** VARIETY

The same grape as *Bastardo,* found in the eastern regions of France.

■ **Valdepenas** (val-duh-PAYN-yuh) VARIETY

In some parts of California, *Tempranillo* goes by the name of this Spanish wine region.

■ **Valpolicella** (val-pole-lee-chel-lah) APPELLATION

The ubiquitous wine of Italy's Veneto region is the region's answer to basic *Chianti*. Made from *Rondinella, Molinara, Corvina* and 4 other grapes, it is a delightful every day quaffer that can show some real character if allowed. Styles range from simple refreshment to serious fireside wines, including *Ripasso* and *Amarone*.

Food Matches Antipasto, charcuterie, sausages, lentils, pasta, parmesan, carbonara, bean salad, tuna salad, mushrooms.

■ **Villard Noir** (vee-yard nwarr) HYBRID

Another French/North American hybrid, this hardy, high yielding vine once covered some 30,000 ha. of French vineyards but, thanks to government incentives, has been grubbed up almost totally. The grape still can be found in isolated pockets of Ontario.

Descriptors Villard Noir produces a lightish wine with good colour, red berry flavours and a slightly tarry aspect, without any trace of foxiness.

■ Vranac   VARIETY

This very old variety is important in the eastern European regions of Macedonia, Serbia and Montenegro. The wine appears in blends with *Cabernet Sauvignon* and *Merlot* and also as a distinctive varietal. Analysis suggests that it may be the offspring of *Plavac Mali,* which would put it in the *Primitivo* and *Zinfandel* family. The name Vranac means black stallion, a reference to the deep colour and strength of the wine.

Descriptors   Deeply coloured, usually with a lot of body and extract, and a tendency toward rustic. The nose presents red berries, black fruits, herbs, cinnamon, chocolate, and liquorice, and usually a woody note from oak ageing, to which the grape has an affinity. High in acid and tannins, the wines can take time to reach their peak.

Food Matches   Smoked, cured or grilled meats; sausages; flavourful cheeses, hunter stew.

■ Xynomavro (TZEE-noh-muh-vroh)   VARIETY

Literally "black acid", this is the great red grape of Greece, and can be found all over that country but nowhere else. Often called Greece's answer to *Cabernet Sauvignon,* the grape produces deep, rich, character-filled wines that are worthy of ageing for up to five years and as much as 15 years. May be blended with other local grapes as well as Cabernet Sauvignon.

Descriptors   Although sometimes coarse in their youth, the wines are fruity, spicy, medium to full bodied, with deep colour, good tannins and a firm acidic bite. Sometimes compared to *Nebbiolo*.

Food Matches   Serve with anything Greek, especially lamb, feta, moussaka, aubergine, goulash.

■ Zinfandel   VARIETY

First documented in the early 1800s, California's Zinfandel has been used to make everything from cheap jug wines to syrupy port-style wines. Zinfandel grows everywhere in California, and is responsible for the popular blush wine called White Zinfandel. Grown high up the valley slopes and treated to quality vineyard management, Zin produces serious wines with rich colour and depth, and very high alcohol – at least 13% and often as high as 16% – that age well for up to 8 years. Now known to be a descendent of the *Primitivo* grape of southern Italy, it can be a great summer wine. (ALSO SEE PLAVAC MALI.)

Descriptors   Zinfandel can be intensely spicy, with aromas of black pepper, blackberries, raspberries and usually oak. Big, powerful and full of character, with a solid layer of tannin. May be treated to Carbonic Maceration.

Food Matches   Antipasti, BBQ sauce, beef stroganoff, chili, curried lamb, dark chocolate, game casserole, pepper steak, moussaka, ratatouille, stuffed peppers, teriyaki, turkey, asiago, old cheddar, gorgonzola, chocolate cake.

■ Zweigelt/Zweigeltrebe   VARIETY
(SVYE-gelt/SVYE-gelt-RAY-beh)

This relative new-comer first appeared in 1922 and has since become very important in Austria. It can be serious and age-worthy with bite and body, but is just as often delicate. Now beginning to appear in Germany, Great Britain and Canada. A cross of *Blaufränkish* and *St. Laurent,* it is also known as Blauer Zweigelt.

Descriptors   Smooth and velvety on the palate, with aromas of fresh raspberries, sour cherries and spice. Fruity when young; smooth and velvety when aged. Can be quite tannic.

Food Matches   Duck, goose, ham, grilled fish, munster, blue cheeses, cheddar, antipasto, tomato sauces, any sort of chicken.

Notes

Notes

Notes

Notes

Notes

Appendix

- **Old World Appellations at a Glance**
- **Glossary of Oenological Terms**
- **Bibliography**
- **Acknowledgements**

Old World Appellations at a Glance

Although the methods of giving a name to wine are few, wine buyers are chronically challenged to figure out what's what. Wines can bear a varietal name, which is the name of the grape or grapes used; a generic name, such as "California Chablis"; a made-up or fantasy name, ranging from "Mountain Rouge" to "Grange" and "Opus One"; and, as is the case with many Old World wine regions, a place name – an appellation – whether a region, village, vineyard, or chateau.

The varietal naming system is the easiest to cope with. If the label says Pinot Gris, then the bottle contains the fermented juice of, predominantly, Pinot Gris grapes. However, in the case of regional names, sorting things out can be a challenge even for the seasoned wine professional. So here is a quick overview of the regions that use or mostly use place names on their labels and the most important grapes that go into their wines. The purpose here is not to provide a comprehensive list of appellations but simply to offer a key to help you find the winegrapes you are interested in or to discover what's behind a wine you have your eye on. (Grapes not included in this book appear in *italics*.)

■ Austria

As a wine producing country, Austria is both under-appreciated and under-represented in the international wine markets. Austria's 18 wine-growing areas produce distinctive, high quality wines, all of which are varietally labelled, however the grape names are often uniquely Austrian. There are three classifications for wine, all based on ripeness at harvest: Tafelwein, Qualitatswein, and Prädikatswein (certified).

White: *Bouvier,* Chardonnay, Grüner-Veltliner, Müller-Thurgau, 'Muskateller', Muskat-Ottonel, *Neuberger,* Riesling, *Rotgipfler,* Sauvignon Blanc, Traminer, Weiserburgunder, Welschriesling.

Red: Blauer Burgunder, *Blauer Portugieser,* Blauer Zweigelt (Rotberger), Blaufrankisch, Cabernet Sauvignon, Merlot, St. Laurent.

■ France

France may legitimately be called the nursery of the "noble" vinifera grapes. Most of the varietal names seen on labels today are of French origin. Yet French wine labels rarely mention grape names. Instead, wines are named for where they were produced, the "correct" grapes for each region having been worked out and written into law long ago. Fortunately, the palette of grapes in any one region is usually small, making that aspect fairly easy to master. The same cannot be said of the complex and often arbitrary system of subregions, departments, villages, vineyards, and classification levels that determines what goes onto French wine labels. In 2007 France embarked on a conversion to a simplified classification system, in keeping with EU standards. The number of wine classes will be reduced and varietal labels will be permitted. Whether this will help or hinder has yet to be determined.

■ *Alsace*

Most Alsace wines bear a varietal name, although a ruling passed in 2005 allows classed growth vineyards to omit the grape name in favour of a regional or winery name only. Alsace wines are mainly dry and usually very high quality.
Classifications: Grand Cru, Appellation Alsace Controllée, Edelzwicker, Zwicker (a lesser blend); also Vendange Tardive, Sélection des Grains Nobles (Noble Rot), and Crémant d'Alsace.
White: Auxerrois, Chasselas, Gewurztraminer, Klevner, Muscat, Pinot Blanc, Pinot Gris (formerly called Tokay d'Alsace), Riesling, Sylvaner.
Red: Pinot Noir.

■ *Bordeaux*

Bordeaux has six districts or departments: Médoc, Graves, Pomerol, St. Emilion, Entre-deux-Mers, and Sauternes (a subregion of Graves). Wineries higher up the quality ladder are entitled to use only the winery name, often with no mention of Bordeaux anywhere on the label. The task of deciphering the wines is aided only somewhat by a small roster of allowed grape varieties. A knowledge of Bordeaux geography, producers and chateaux is pretty much required here.

Classifications: Premier Grand Cru, Grand Cru, Premier Cru through Cinqieme Cru, Appellation Bordeaux Controllée, Vin de Pays.

White: Columbard, Folle Blanche, Muscadelle, Sauvignon Blanc, Semillon.

Red: Cabernet Franc, Cabernet Sauvignon, Carmenère, Malbec (Cot), Merlot, Petite Verdot.

■ Burgundy

As in Bordeaux, Burgundians prefer to name their wines after either the appellation or the producer (often a "shipper"). The palate of grapes is even smaller than in Bordeaux. Burgundy has five districts: Chablis, Côte d'Or (made up of Côte de Nuit and Côte de Beaune), Côte Chalonnais, Maconnaise, and Beaujolais. Varietal names appear occasionally. Note that white Burgundy and Beaujolais are made from Chardonnay, and red Beaujolais is 100% Gamay.

Classifications: Premier Grand Cru, Grand Cru, Premiere Cru, Villages, Petite (as in Petite Chablis), AC Bourgogne, Passetoutgrains, Crémant de Bourgogne.

White: Aligoté, Chardonnay, Pinot Blanc, Pinot Gris.

Red: Gamay, Pinot Noir.

■ Champagne

While Champagne produces a limited amount of still wine for local consumption, it is the world's foremost producer and exporter of premium sparkling wines. The regional name is controlled but only appears in the fine print on the label. Champagne is normally named for the producer or "house", and each house has its own quality tiers. A champagne house that grows its own grapes is rare. Instead, grapes are classified prior to their sale to the champagne makers.

White/Rosé: Chardonnay, Pinot Noir, Pinot Meunier.

Blanc de Blanc: Chardonnay.

Blanc de Noirs: Pinot Noir, Pinot Meunier.

■ Languedoc-Rousillon

Once written off as France's "wine lake", the region is now a major player in the fine wine market. Names such as Banyuls, Corbiéres, Faugéres, Minervois, and St. Chinion are becoming regulars in wine dealers' catalogues. As well, varietal wines under the Vin de Pays designation are delivering unprecedented value, with winemakers happy to grow just about anything.

White: Bourboulenc, Chardonnay, Chenin Blanc, Clairette Blanche, Grenache Blanc, Maccabeo, Malvoisie, Marsanne, Muscat, Picpoul, Roussane, Sauvignon Blanc, Ugni Blanc, Vermentino.

Red: Cabernet Franc, Cabernet Sauvignon, Carignan, Cinsaut, Gamay, Grenache, Malbec, Merlot, Mourvedre, Syrah.

▪ Loire Valley

Straddling the Loire River from just west of Champagne to the Atlantic coast, the Loire Valley has 14 wine regions and includes many that are household names: Anjou, Saumur, Bourgueil, Cheverny, Chinon, Poitou, Muscadet, Pouilly Fumé, Quarts De Chaume, Quincy, Reuilly, Sancerre, Touraine, Vouvray.

Classifications: Appellation d'Origin, Vin Delimité de Qualité Supérieur, Vin de Pays, Vin de Pays de Zone.

White: Chardonnay, Chenin Blanc, Muscadet (Melon de Bourgonia), Muscat, Pinot Gris, Sauvignon Blanc.

Red: Cabernet Franc, Gamay, *Groslot,* Malbec, Pinot Noir.

▪ Rhône Valley

Hugging the Rhône River from just south of Burgundy almost to the Mediterranean, the Rhône valley has been under vine for well over 2000 years. There are 21 allowed grapes in the region's 6 departments and 163 communes, but the area's top red wines – Hermitage, Châteauneuf-du-Pape, and Côtes du Rhône – rely mainly or exclusively on Syrah and Grenache. Wines from anywhere outside of the principal areas fall under the general Côtes du Rhône class. Although less plentiful, corresponding Rhône white wines are often very good value.

Regions: *Northern Rhône* – Côte Rhotie, Condrieu, Chateau Grillet, St. Joseph, Crozes Hermitage, Cornas, St. Peray.

Southern Rhône – Gigondas, Vacqueyras, Châtauneuf-du-Pape, Lirac, Tavel.

Classifications: Côtes du Rhône Cru, Côtes du Rhône Villages, Côtes du Rhône.

White: Bourboulenc, Chardonnay, Clairette, *Gross Plant,* Marsanne, Muscat, Picpoul, Roussanne, Sauvignon Blanc, Semillon, Ugni Blanc, Vermentino, Viognier.

Red: Carignan, Cinsaut, Gamay, Grenache, Mourvèdre, Pinot Noir, Petite Sirah, Syrah.

■ Germany

German vineyards occupy some of Europe's most northerly and coolest wine-growing areas. Vineyards tend to hug the rivers, especially the Rhine, and are often planted on slopes so steep they can only be worked by hand. The German classification system is based on grape ripeness at harvest, since ripeness is an issue at this northerly growing limit. German wines have a rich tradition of off-dry, semi-dry, and sweet wines, although dry wines are becoming more popular. Despite the complexity of German wine labels, the bottle will always include a varietal name. To add a bit of confusion, a 2002 regulation allowed the "Classic" and "Selection" designations, accompanied by little explanation of what those tags mean.

Major Regions: Mosel-Saar-Ruwer, Nahe, Rheingau, Rhein-hessen, Rheinpfalz (Palatinate).

Minor Regions: Ahr, Baden, Franken/Franconia, Hessische Bergstrasse, Mittelrhein, Wurttemberg.

Classifications: Tafelwein; Deutscher Tafelwein; Qualitatswein (QbA); Qualitatswein mit Pradikat (QmP), which includes, in order of increasing ripeness, Kabinett, Spatlese, Aüslese, plus the QmP sweet wines Beerenauslese and Trockenbeeren-auslese; Eiswein; and Sekt, a sparkling wine.

White: Bacchus, Elbling, *Goldriesling,* Grauburgunder, Kern-er, Müller-Thurgau, Riesling, *Rivaner,* Scheurebe, Sylvaner, Weisburgunder.

Red: Dornfelder, Lemberger, Portugeiser, Schwarzriesling (Pi-not Meunier), Spätburgunder, St. Laurent, Trollinger.

■ Italy

Italy's rich wine tradition is based on a dizzying array of grapes (more than 800 varieties), many of which are indigen-ous to a single region, although international grapes are also planted. Labelling conventions are divided between regional names and varietal names. In Piedmont, for example, Barolo and Barbaresco are named after their towns of origin, whereas Cortese and Barbera are grape names. While most regions use some varietal names (Abruzzi and Basilicatta use only varietal names), the result is a perplexing mix of village names and indigenous grapes.

Regions: Abruzzi, Basilicatta, Calabria, Campania, Emilia-Romagna, Friuli, Latium, Liguria, Lombardy, Marche, Molise, Piedmont, Sardinia, Sicily, Trentino/Alto-Adige, Tuscany, Umbria, Valle d'Aosta, Veneto.

Classifications: Vino da Tavola, Vina Typica, Indicacione de Geografica Typica (IGT), Denominationi di Origine Controllata (DOC), DOC Guarantita (DOCG). Also Classico, Riserva & Superiore.

White: Albana, Arneis, *Aromatica, Bambino Bianco,* Canaiolo, Catarratto, Chardonnay, Cortese, Garganega, Greco, Malvoisie, Moscato, Müller-Thurgau, Pinot Bianco, Pinot Grigio, Prosecco, Riesling Italico, Roussanne, Sauvignon Blanc, Semillon, Sylvaner, (Tocai) Friulano, Trebbiano, Verdello, Verdicchio, Vermentino.

Red: Aglianico, Barbera, *Bonarda,* Brunello, Cabernet Franc, Cabernet Sauvignon, *Calabrese,* Canaiolo, Carignano, Cesanese, Corvina, *Croatina,* Dolcetto, Freisa, Gamay, Grignolino, *Lagrein,* Lambrusco, Malbec, Malvasia, Merlot, *Molinara,* Montepulciano, Nebbiolo, *Negrara,* Nero D'Avola, Pignolo, Pinot Nero, Primitivo, Refosco, Rondinella, Sangiovese, *Sangioveto, Schiava,* Syrah.

■ Portugal

Portugal has nine designated wine growing regions, many of which grow mainly little-known indigenous grapes (there are 41 grape varieties in Vinho Verde alone). Like many Old World wine-producing countries, Portugal has an appellation system that controls place names and how they may be applied. Varietal labels are beginning to appear.

Regions: Vinho Verde, Douro (Porto), Dao, Bairraida, Buçelas, Colares, Concavelos, Setubel, Algarve.

Classifications: Denomination of Controlled Origin (DCO), Indication of Origin Regulated (IOR), Regional Wine. Also: Vinho Verde, Vino de Mesa, Garrafeira (aged 2 years), Madeira, Porto.

White: Alvarinho, Arinto, Bical, Boal, Borrado das Moscas, Cercial, *Encruzado, Fernâo Pires,* Loureiro, Malvasia, Moscatel, Verdelho.

Red: *Alfrocheiro,* Alicante Bouschet, *Aragonez,* Arinto, Baga, Bastardo, Cabernet Sauvignon, *Negra Mole,* Periquita, *Tinta Borroca,* Tinta Roriz, Touriga Franca, Touriga Nacional, *Trincadeira.*

■ Spain

When the Romans arrived in the Iberian Peninsula, vineyards were already well established. Today Spain ranks first in acreage under vine, but being almost desert, it ranks third in total wine production. Spain has 18 demarcated wine regions, only a few of which are well known, and grows a reported 600 grape varieties. Most are indigenous, although international varieties are beginning to appear. With a few exceptions, bottles carry a regional name.

Regions: *North* – Priorato, Tarragona, Penédes, Somontano, Cariñena, Navarra, Rioja, Ribera del Duero, Rueda, Toro, Rias Baixas.

South – La Mancha, Valdepeñas, Montilla-Morilly, Jerez, Malaga, Valencia, Utiel-Requena.

Classifications: Vino de Mesa, Guarantita de Origin, Denominación de Origen (DO), Denominación De Origen Calificada (DOC). Also Vino Joven (aged 1 year), Vino de Crianza (aged 2 years), Reserva (aged 3 years), Gran Reserva (aged 5 years); Cava; Sherry.

White: Airen, Albarino, Bual, Chardonnay, Chenin Blanc, Folle Blanche, Garnacha Blanca, Loureiro, Macabeo, Malvasia, Moscatel, Palomino, Parellada, Sauvignon Blanc, Torrontés, Verdejo, Pedro Ximemez, Verdelho, Viura, Xarel-Lo.

Red: Bastardo Negro, Bobal, Cabernet Sauvignon, Cariñena, Cencibel, Garnacha Tinta, Graciano, Loureiro Tinta, Merlot, Monastrell, *Moscatel Negro,* Syrah, Tempranillo, Tinto Fino.

■ Eastern Europe

The majority of Eastern European wines bear a varietal name, but the names are often indigenous local variations, sometimes with the addition of a regional name.

Glossary of Oenological Terms

Acid/Acidic

Fresh, tart or sour character caused by good acids. Important for body and longevity in white wines. Plays an important but less obvious role in the structure of red wines.

Appellation

French legal term meaning place name.

Black Grapes

Dark-skinned grapes that produce red wines. Skins are actually dark blue or dark purple, and give off colouring during *maceration*.

Blend

A wine that is blended from any combination of grapes, vineyards, appellations or vintages. Ranges from adding Merlot to Cabernet to soften a rich Bordeaux, to mixing cheap bulk wines to produce a branded jug wine. Most wines are a blend of some sort.

Bocksbeutal

A "flagon" shaped bottle, popular in Franken and Portugal, said to have been fashioned after a certain part of the anatomy of a male goat.

Botrytis Cinerea

Technically grey rot, but when conditions are right it becomes *noble rot,* which shrivels grapes and condenses sugars, flavours and acids. Botrytized grapes produce luscious dessert wines.

Carbonic Maceration

A fermentation technique popular in Beaujolais in which whole grapes are fermented in closed tanks, releasing juice under their own weight. The resulting wine tends to be light, fresh and fruity.

Cava

Spanish term for *traditional method* sparkling wines made from traditional grapes. Considered an appellation although several regions use the term.

Champagne Method/Methode Champenoise

The original term for bottle-fermented sparkling wine, but was outlawed for general use by the EU in 1994. All wine-producing regions must now use the term Traditional Method. May indicate "Fermented in this bottle" on the label.

Charmat

A technique of producing sparkling wine by inducing a second fermentation in a closed tank rather than a bottle. Produces good sparkling wines at a moderate price.

Chateau

Bordelaise term for a wine-growing estate.

Estate Wine

A wine that is grown, vinified and bottled on a single estate and usually bearing the name of the estate. A sign of quality. (A.k.a. Chateau Bottled, Domaine Bottled.)

Fermentation

A complex, natural process whereby yeasts feed on the sugars in grape juice in an anaerobic environment and create alcohol and CO_2. Also facilitates the development of the aromas and flavours that characterize wine.

Foxy

Aroma/flavour found in North American Labrusca or "fox" grapes, similar to Concord grape juice. Caused by methyl anthranilate, which is found in many North American grape species.

Icewine/Eiswein

Wine that is made from frozen grapes harvested at -8 degrees celcius or lower. Icewines are extremely sweet, honeyed and flavourful.

Late Harvest

Indicates that the grapes were left on the vine several weeks after normal harvest time. Tends to substantially increase sugars and flavours. Not necessarily sweet.

Lees/Sur Lie

Indicates that the wine spent time in contact with dead yeast cells, which adds to character and can impart a light prickle.

Maceration

Refers to the time red grape must spends on the skins to extract colour, flavour and tannin during the first phase of fermentation.

Malolactic Fermentation/Malo

A secondary bacterial fermentation that converts tart malic acid to softer lactic acid. A common practice with many red wines and Chardonnay.

Marc/Pomace

Grape solids – skins, seeds and sometimes stems – remaining after pressing wine must. Sometimes used to create a second wine or spirit (e.g. Grappa di Marc).

Must

Literally "new", must is the fresh grape juice (and solids, in the case of red grapes) that is to be fermented into wine.

New World

1. Any wine-growing region that is not part of Old World Europe;
2. A style of gung-ho wine-making that emphasizes technology and bucking tradition.

Nouveau

French for "new", as in Beaujolais Nouveau.

Noble Grape

One of a small number of grapes valued for the quality of the wines they produce (Cabernet, Chardonnay, Pinot Noir, and Sauvignon Blanc, among others).

Noble Rot

Colloquial term for the beneficial form of Botrytis. (French: Pourriture Noble; German: Edelfäule.)

Old Vines

An unregulated term that can mean as little as 15 years but usually means 30- to 60-year-old vines. Grapevines begin producing acceptable winegrapes after their fourth year and can live 100 years or more. Many produce their best – and fewest – grapes when "old". Sometimes called ancient vines.

Old World

1. The traditional wine-growing countries of Europe including France, Italy, Germany, Austria, Spain, Portugal, and Switzerland;
2. A style of winemaking that focuses on terroir, tradition and finesse.

Organic

1. Environmentally friendly viticultural practices that eschew chemicals in favour of soil building using compost, manure and cover crops;
2. A wine that has been grown and produced using organic methods.

Over-cropping

Allowing vines to produce too many grapes resulting in wines that are hollow, watery and characterless.

Phylloxera Vastatrix

A microscopic North American aphid that feeds on the roots of grapevines. Responsible for destroying most of Europe's vineyards in the late 1800s. North American vines and hybrids are mostly immune and are used as rootstock for virtually all grapevines today.

QWPSR

A European Union specification meaning Quality Wine Produced in a Specified Region to differentiate locally-grown regional or country wines from blended table wines.

Recioto (It.)

Wine made from dried or partially dried (raisined) grapes taken from the "ears" of the cluster to make the dense red wine known as Amarone.

Ripasso

A wine that has been fermented on the left-over marc of another wine, imparting some of the qualities specific to the marc.

Second Label

If the finished wine is not up to the vintner's top quality, it may be bottled and sold under a lesser label (e.g. Les Forts de Latour is the second label of Chateau Latour).

Sekt

German sparkling wine usually made by the *transfer method* using noble grapes.

Single Vineyard

New World equivalent of estate wine, where 100% of the grapes came from the same property. An indicator of high quality, high price or both.

Tannin(s)

A group of compounds derived from skins, pips, stalks and barrels that cause astringency and sometimes bitterness. Provide grip, structure and a drying effect in reds. Important for clarifying and creating deposits during ageing. Tannins are considered out of place in white wines.

Teinturier

Most grapes have a pale green or almost colourless pulp under the skin. Teinturier grapes have red pulp and juice and are mainly used to add colour to a pale red wine.

Terroir (Fr.)

The theory that where the grapes are grown is all-important to the quality of the wine. Includes the soil, subsoil, elevation, weather, climate, mesoclimate, microclimate, drainage, and aspect.

Traditional Method

Internationally accepted term for sparkling wines made by the "champagne method" where a second fermentation is induced in the same bottle the wine will be sold in.

Typicity

Refers to how typical a wine is of its grape, style, vintage, and region.

Varietal

A wine that is named after its major grape, although it may contain as little as 75% of that grape blended with 25% "other" (subject to local laws).

V.D.Q.S.

Vin Delimité de Qualité Superiore, a little-used French classification for wines one rung below AOC in quality.

Vendange Tardive

The term used in Alsace for Late Harvest.

Vintage

1. The wine-making process, the harvest, or the crop;

2. The year in which the grapes were harvested (although many jurisdictions allow up to 15% from another vintage). A vintage designation suggests a higher level of quality;

3. A wine of the highest quality. Sometimes a vintage is "declared" in exceptional years in a region where blending vintages is the norm, e.g. champagne, port.

Wine

Although almost anything can be used to make wine, some jurisdictions define it exclusively as the fermented juice of grapes.

Yeast

Single-celled organisms related to algae and fungi that feed on sugars to produce carbon dioxide and alcohol. (Alcohol is actually produced by a complex series of reactions caused by enzymes that the yeasts produce.)

Yield

Amount of wine produced from a given area of vineyard. Low yields produce better quality wines; high yields (over-cropping) produce watery wines.

Bibliography

While I have relied on a broad range of resources, I must acknowledge the special role of Jancis Robinson and her indispensable book, *Jancis Robinson's Guide to Wine Grapes*. Its importance here cannot be over emphasized. That said, I have also relied extensively on the following, as well as my own tasting notes.

Barty-King, Hugh. *A Taste of English Wine*. London: Pelham Books, 1989

Broadbent, Michael. *Michael Broadbent's Winetasting*. London: Mitchell Beazley, 2000

Burroughs, D. & Bezzant, N. *Wine Regions of the World,* 2nd edition. Oxford: Wine & Spirit Education Trust, 1988

Clarke, Oz. *Oz Clarke's Introducing Wine*. New York: Harcourt Books, 2000

Clarke, Oz & Rand, Margaret. *Oz Clarke's Encyclopedia of Grapes*. New York: Harcourt Inc, 2001

Cox, Jill & Lord, Tony. *Which Food Which Wine*. Bristol: Andre Deutsch, 1990

Darling, Shari. *Harmony on the Palate*. Vancouver: Whitecap Books, 2005

Galet, Pierre. *Grape Varieties*. London: Cassell Illustrated, 2002

Hazan, Victor. *Italian Wine*. New York: Alfred A. Knopf, 1982

Johnson-Bell, Linda. *Good Food Fine Wine*. London: Cassell/Orion Publishing, 1999

Robinson, Jancis. *Jancis Robinson's Guide to Wine Grapes*. Oxford: Oxford University Press, 1996

Robinson, Jancis. Vines, Grapes & Wines. London: Mitchell Beazley, 1999

Sharp, Andrew. *Winetaster's Secrets*. Toronto: Warwick Publishing, 1996

Simon, Joanna. *Wine with Food*. New York: Simon & Shuster, 1996

Zraly, Kevin. *Windows On The World Complete Wine Course*. New York: Sterling Publishing, 1999

Acknowledgements

I would like to thank fellow wine
writers Dean Tudor and Dr. David
Goldberg for their assistance in
checking the details.

Index

Notes